DICK WALKER

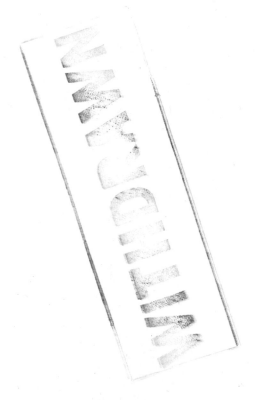

By the same author
Still-Water Angling

DICK WALKER'S ANGLING

Theories and Practice,
Past, Present and to Come

With a foreword by Peter Maskell

ANGLING TIMES
in association with
DAVID & CHARLES
Newton Abbot London North Pomfret (Vt)

0715 378 147 1158

British Library Cataloguing in Publication Data

Walker, Richard, b.1918
Dick Walker's angling.
1. Fishing
I. Title   II. 'Angling times'
799.1'2   SH439

ISBN 0–7153–7814–7

Photoset and printed in Great Britain
by Redwood Burn Limited, Trowbridge & Esher
for David & Charles (Publishers) Limited
Brunel House   Newton Abbot   Devon

Published in the United States of America
by David & Charles Inc
North Pomfret   Vermont   05053 USA

799.12
w15

JN 4920

Contents

Foreword

Angling remains one of the few sports where the use of the superlative retains any real credibility. On football pitch or golf course the capable performer may be transformed overnight into a 'star'; the gifted into a 'superstar' or 'world-beater'. When the gulf between fact and fiction, man and myth, is eventually exposed the search begins again for a new Man of the Moment. Fortunately angling is not a glamorous sport where 'stars' are manufactured overnight. It is essentially for the practical, a sport where respect must be earned the hard way—by results. Few men in the entire history of the sport are as widely respected as Dick Walker. Not even the meanest-minded angler would deny his ability and achievements. For the last quarter of a century Dick Walker has dominated the angling spectrum both through his writing and his angling exploits. It could be argued that other great anglers are equally skilled; that may well be true. It is equally true, however, that no other living angler combines instinctive ability with Walker's scientific approach, his ability to analyse an angling problem and solve it by using his commonsense.

He became a fisherman, way back in 1922, at the tender age of four. Encouraged by his grandfather, also named Richard, he soon learned the basic techniques of coarse fishing, and a great deal more besides about plants, animals, fish, insects, and the rest of the waterside wildlife. He was educated at the Friends School, Saffron Walden and St Christopher School, Letchworth. After reading Engineering at Caius College, Cambridge, he was involved in airborne radar during World War II. When that was over he returned to regular fishing and writing about it, first for *The Angler's News* and *Fishing Gazette* and later for *Angling Times*. His engineering background has helped a great deal in his rod and tackle designing—he is design consultant for Hardy Brothers of Alnwick—and he is also a director of a firm which manufactures lawn-mowers.

It was Dick Walker, who, together with a handful of like-minded angling friends, first tackled the catching of specimen carp in a scientific way. The result was the capture of a 44lb carp, a fish of almost unbelievable proportions to the angling world of the 'Fifties. His carp record has stood since 1952. But more significantly the capture of that fish led to a complete reversal of angling attitudes. Anglers began to realize that big fish were caught not by luck but by angling skill and commonsense. The carp became a cult fish, attracting thousands of devotees and the specimen hunter and the angler who enlists science as well as technique in his pursuit of big fish, was born.

Dick Walker's list of specimen fish makes fascinating reading and I think it is worth recording at least some of them, for his modesty matches his expertise: perch – eight over 4lb; dace – seven over 1lb; barbel – about fifty double-figure; chub – about fifty over 6lb; roach – hundreds from 2lb to 3lb 4oz; bream – dozens over 8lb; trout – twenty over 10lb and up to $18\frac{1}{4}$lb (including two double-figure brown trout and an 18lb rainbow trout); tench – hundreds over 5lb; rudd – hundreds over 2lb and up to 3lb 3oz; pike – several of 20lb; eels – up to $5\frac{3}{4}$lb; salmon – up to 28lb; carp – hundreds over 10lb, not to mention 44lb 'Clarissa'; grayling – up to 2lb 14oz.

Since 1953 Dick has passed on all the skill and knowledge that led to the capture of those big fish to millions of anglers. When *Angling Times* was first launched, twenty-five years ago, Dick was asked to write a weekly column. He accepted and has been writing for the paper ever since. His columns, a blend of instruction, commonsense, and humour, have done much to raise the standard of angling to its present-day level. His simple, down-to-earth style reflects the straightforward nature of the man, his genuine desire to pass on his knowledge to both beginner and experienced angler. His achievements in this respect are remarkable. It was Dick who first produced the Arlesey bomb, now the most widely used leger lead in coarse fishing. It was Dick who first produced the electric bite alarm; the Grinner and double Grinner knots. It was Dick who first predicted, way back in the 'Fifties, that the National Championship would one day be won by a leger angler; it was Dick who first examined in detail the relationship between water temperature and the feeding habits of fish. The list of Walker firsts is endless. Even in a world of hackneyed superlatives, he is quite simply The Best. This book contains the best from The Best, a selection of articles which are as relevant now as the day they were written.

Peter Maskell   January 1979

Part One:
Thoughts in General

1 I say again, hooked fish don't feel pain

The decision by the RSPCA to press for angling to be prohibited, on the grounds that it is cruel, is something that no angler can take lightly. Lots of people who held no opinion on the matter before, are now going to say to themselves and to others: 'If the RSPCA, which HM the Queen supports, says fishing is cruel, then cruel it must be!' So it may be a good idea, at this time, to see what answer we can give to people who call us callous, cruel brutes, and are willing to misrepresent the facts and do anything they can think of to convince people that our sport should be stopped.

It is no argument to say that the RSPCA rarely lifts a finger to protect fish. This is true, as we all know. When public authorities and nationalized industries decide to bury fish alive under domestic refuse or fly ash, it is always anglers who go to the rescue. Did you ever hear of a prosecution by the RSPCA in such a case? As far as they're concerned, it's cruel to put the fish on the bank, but quite all right to put the bank on the fish.

At the same time, it's no good saying that because others treat fish cruelly, we anglers ought to be able to do the same. It might be better to explain that if you want to see cruelty to fish, you should take a few trips on commercial fishing vessels. There you will see hooks removed from the stomachs of fish caught on long lines, by putting a foot on the fish and pulling on the line till the hook and, often, some of the fish's guts, comes away. You may also see fish gutted alive and thrown into troughs, still kicking.

The RSPCA takes no action against this though I have no doubt that many of those of its members who voted to abolish angling, often eat fish so caught and treated. But the RSPCA argument is that commercial fishermen do it for their livings, whereas anglers do it for fun. That's what makes the difference. You can treat fish as cruelly as you like as long as you're paid for it, but if you catch them for pleasure, even if you treat them as humanely as possible, you're cruel.

To judge from what Miss Brigid Brophy said when the

matter was debated on the Frost programme on TV, part of the argument against angling is that man has no right to kill anything. Miss Brophy was evidently unaware of the fact that the majority of the fish that anglers catch are not in fact killed, but returned alive to the water; but of course we do kill some that are good to eat.

It would be interesting to know whether Miss Brophy wants to change the RSPCA into a branch of the Vegetarian Society; but if the majority of her fellow RSPCA members take the view that it is permissible to eat fish, then one can point out the sheer foolishness of their position. It is quite ridiculous to say that it is cruel for an angler to kill a fish humanely, but quite all right if he eats a fish that has been cruelly killed by someone paid to catch and kill it.

The real issue, however, is whether or not it is cruel to catch a fish by sticking a hook in its mouth.

During the TV debate, I explained that some fish will eat quantities of sticklebacks. The commonest kind of stickleback has three long, hard, sharp dorsal spines and two others, equally long, hard, and sharp, sticking out from its sides. Other fish grab these highly prickly creatures in their mouths, swallow them, and carry them in their stomachs till they're digested. I have found as many as forty sticklebacks in a trout's stomach.

In some waters, caddis grubs use, among other things, hard, sharp thorns to make their cases. All kinds of fish swallow these grubs, case and all. It is by no means rare to find that one or more of the thorns has pierced the stomach wall of a fish, which nevertheless is entirely fit and healthy.

I refuse absolutely to believe that fish that eat objects as hard as thorns and stickleback spines, can suffer pain from being caught on a fish hook. But when I made this point, Miss Brophy put forward a cunning, if specious argument. She said: 'If you have to operate on a baby and find a safety pin in its stomach, would you argue that babies can safely swallow safety pins?' I didn't get the chance to reply to that at the time, Frost programme debates being trials by shouting-matches, so I'll answer it now. Babies don't feed regularly and grow fat on safety pins, but fish do feed regularly and grow fat on caddises and sticklebacks.

I am absolutely convinced that fish feel no pain when they are hooked. Nor do I believe that they feel terror, in the sense that we know it. They find themselves tethered and they do their best to get rid of the encumbrance. There is no more cruelty in it than in lassoing a horse.

All of us who have fished for any length of time have encountered instances where fish have survived injuries that would be agonizing and fatal to warm-blooded animals. If a cat or a cow gets a hook in its stomach, it will suffer and die. To a fish, it isn't even an inconvenience. I caught a small trout once that had swallowed the hook, so I cut the nylon and let the fish go. Two years later I caught that trout again. I discovered the fact by finding my hook inside it, because the trout had grown big enough to be eatable in the interval and I killed it and took it home.

Then there was the case of the pike that swallowed a live rat which tried to gnaw its way out of the pike's stomach. It had got as far as its shoulders, with its head projecting out of the pike, when the pike took an angler's spoon and was caught.

Nobody who has seen cases like these is going to believe that fish suffer pain through being caught on rod, line, and hook. Unfortunately, most members of the public know nothing about fish, nor do they want to go fishing. Many are likely to support attempts to ban it, since they have nothing to lose.

One more thing. It is argued that there is no need for anyone to go fishing. No man need starve if he can't catch fish himself, and is not therefore justified in catching them for enjoyment. Nowadays, it is still assumed by politicians and others that if you give people enough material things, feed them, clothe them, and look after their physical health, they'll be happy. Sweden, the most advanced country in the world by that standard, has also the highest suicide and mental illness rates. Men have deep-rooted instincts that prompt them to go out and hunt. If they can't, look out for trouble. Look out for riots, look out for hooliganism at football matches. Look out for all sorts of violence and anti-social behaviour.

I cannot accept the argument that a man mustn't enjoy catching a fish, but can be allowed to enjoy eating it. As millions of anglers regularly prove, the first is more important to happiness in our civilization than the second.

2 Selling is a dirty word

Why should an angler who catches trout from a reservoir be condemned for selling his catch? To hear some of the talk that is rife nowadays one would think that to do this is the worst of all angling crimes. The most charitable construction I can place on the motives of the critics is that they don't understand the management of a trout-stocked reservoir.

The reason for stocking a water supply reservoir is not simply to provide anglers with recreation. A reservoir left to itself produces very large quantities of algae. On this, various creatures feed. They include snails, insects and crustacea. Most of them present the water engineers with a purification problem, in that either filters become clogged, or solid matter emerges from household taps, or the water tastes horrible, or a combination of these nuisances.

This problem is reduced if trout are put into the reservoir; they eat up some of the animals, put on weight, and are then caught by anglers and taken away. By the amount of weight they have gained, the problem of removing solid matter from the water is reduced. Consequently angling rules are formulated to encourage this overall effect.

What is wanted is a system of putting in fish about 9 or 10 in long and then taking them out after they've grown by a reasonable amount, say to 12in.

Regulate stocking

So we have sets of rules that regulate the rate at which trout are removed, the size at which they may be taken, and so on. At Grafham, the rules say that you must kill every fish you catch over 12in long, up to a limit of eight fish. The management, by insisting on catch returns, knows what the rate of removal is, and can regulate this rate either by varying the rules from time to time, or by altering the stocking programme.

It can therefore be seen that, so far from being wrong to take fish away from a water managed in this way, it is highly desirable to do so. The management, in fact, insists on it.

Now, by adopting a policy of stocking reservoirs with trout, water undertakings have brought good trout fishing within reach of many more anglers than could formerly afford it; but there remain some to whom a fee of £1 a day,* plus travelling and tackle costs, represents a significant slice of their income.

I can see no reason whatever why anglers in that position shouldn't sell their catches to help pay for their sport, which they might otherwise be unable to afford. An angler who abides by the angling rules must kill and take away the fish he catches, up to the bag limit. It makes not the least difference to the sport or the prospects of sport of other anglers, whether he sells these fish, gives them away, puts them in the dustbin, or buries them under the rose bushes.

It strikes me as odd in the extreme that most of the protests about selling trout seem to emanate from those who are immediately up in arms at the suggestion that rod licence fees, fishery rents, rates, or day ticket costs should ever be increased. 'The working man is being priced out of his fishing!' they cry. But if the working man uses his angling skill to catch and sell a few trout, to help pay for fishing he might otherwise be hard put to afford, he's a bad sportsman and should be barred, beaten, even hanged, if some people had their way. If a professional netsman, a working man, on a salmon river makes a living netting and selling salmon, that's all right. The fishermen of England, toilers of the deep, cod liver oil ads, and our great maritime tradition, hooray! If a man of modest means pays several hundred pounds for a beat on the Dee or Tweed, invites two or three friends to share it, and they come out of the deal only £50 out of pocket, as is pretty commonly done, that's all right.

So what's so desperately wrong about selling a few trout from Grafham or Chew or Weir Wood or any other reservoir if it helps some chap to get a bit of sport who couldn't otherwise afford it?

Perhaps the notion that it is wrong to kill and take away fish stems from the state of most of our coarse fisheries, where there is virtually no management at all and where it is commonly supposed that if most, if not all, of the fish caught weren't returned alive, there would be hardly any left.

* Now £3.50 and likely to increase

15

I sometimes wonder, however, if the real reason behind the wholesale condemnation of the taking away of fish isn't the subconscious thought: 'If that basket hadn't taken those fish away, they'd still be there for me to catch!'

Anglers protested

It is rather similar to the attitude of those who, at the end of last season, protested that there should be a limit on the number of anglers allowed to fish at Grafham. When on the opening day of this season, some of these were turned away because a limit had been set and reached, they were furious. They never meant that a limit should be imposed that would stop them fishing. What they meant was that they wanted fewer other anglers on the water, when they chose to fish.

Perhaps a cool examination of motives might do a lot of good. Are the objections really to the taking and selling of fish, or is there annoyance on the part of some because others have caught fish that they couldn't?

3 How to talk about fishing the hard way

Dry-fly fishing for trout is an exciting and interesting branch of angling, about which more nonsense has been written than any other. Only the other day I read an article whose author said that this was the only branch of angling that could really be called scientific. It might be nearer the mark to say that it's the easiest to sound scientific about!

'Studying the surface, I noticed several specimens of *Baetis rhodani* in the sub-imago state emerging from their nymphal shucks, while at one point I felt sure I could see examples of *Ephemerella ignita*, and this diagnosis was confirmed by the kidney-shaped rise forms.'

That's the kind of stuff to write if you want to make dry-fly fishing sound scientific. What it means is that the chap saw a few Dark Olives about and maybe Blue-winged Olives, too. Or in even simpler terms, there were some little flies, some with dun wings and olive-green bodies and others with dark slaty wings and emerald-green bodies.

Work up your entomological (bug-hunting) jargon and you can sound highly scientific. It isn't very difficult because the study of those insects that are of use to a fly-fisher is only a tiny fraction of the whole vast field of insect study. A kid of ten could learn enough in a few weeks to be on chatting terms with most of the 'expert' fly-fishers.

Of course, if you have a good collection of feathers and have learned the simple craft of tying a trout fly, you don't need to know that the fly you've picked off the water is called a *Leptophlebia vespertina* (imago), or even that its ordinary name is a Claret dun spinner. The trout won't know, anyway! You just have a good look at the little fellow, and then tie the best imitation you can of him (or her). From that point onwards, even the appearance of science begins to fade. You tie this imitation fly on the end of your cast, and you go and look for a rising trout. Now if there should be one rising, no very scientific process is needed to ascertain this fact. You can see it.

Depending upon the nature of the water where the trout is, and between it and you; and also upon such things as wind force and direction, distance to be cast, and so on, putting the fly on the water so that the trout will take it may demand just a little or a very great deal of skill.

In the most difficult cases, it is true to say that there is no other branch of angling that demands more skill, and few that demand as much. But it is skill that is demanded, not science. If you're worried about the difference between skill and science, as well you may be if you read what our national sports writers offer, perhaps I can explain it by saying that a well-trained chimpanzee can display enormous skill, but no matter how well you train it, it will never show the remotest scientific ability.

There is, of course, scope for science in the design of rods and reels for dry-fly-fishing—especially reels, whose design has stagnated for a hundred years—but none of this need be studied by the dry-fly-fisher, who usually takes the design of his tackle for granted and believes implicitly the curious state-

17

ments often put out by the tackle-makers, the result of which is that he will happily pay twice as much for a 9ft two-piece split-cane fly rod, as he would be asked for a 12ft three-piece roach rod, of the same material, which had cost about twice as much to manufacture.

Nowadays, a few dry-fly-fishers who wish to appear learned material, which had cost about twice as much to manufacture.

Nowadays, a few dry-fly-fishers who wish to appear learned, will talk in terms of a peculiar and complicated formula for designating lines, and I am sure they have a lot of fun with it. There's a lovely mixture of letters and figures and grams or grains and what not, which all adds up to the fact that all decent dry-fly rods take a No 3 double-taper silk line.*

Indeed, fly-fishing terminology has grown to the stage were one has to be careful about using it. Such terms as 'stripping guide', 'forward taper', and 'butt-action' do not refer to activities in Soho; but it is so easy to be misunderstood.

By comparison, many aspects of coarse fishing and of salmon fishing are much more scientific. The design of floats, leger-leads, spinning-leads, plugs, and devons offers great scope for scientific thinking. Fixed-spool reels and multipliers need much more scientific engineering than do fly-reels.

The choice of method, whether in salmon fishing or coarse fishing, involves, or can involve, scientific study of water conditions. Temperature, flow-rate, colour, and depth can be measured and from their measurement can be deduced the location and the behaviour of fish.

Whether the degree to which science can be used in a branch of angling is in any way a measure of the merits of that branch is open to doubt. It probably depends upon the nature of the individual angler.

To me, dry-fly-fishing is something I greatly enjoy. To some anglers it is the best of all kinds of fishing; and it might prove so to many more if they were not put off trying it by fools who, to enhance their own angling status, hold it up as the pinnacle of angling ambition, beyond the capabilities of any but the keenest intellect combined with the skill of a master conjuror.

Rubbish! The only difficult thing about dry-fly-fishing is finding an opportunity to practise it.

* Now No 6 AFTM plastic

Part Two:
Tactics

4 Pick a float that grips the water

I did more long-trotting than usual towards the end of last season, mainly because I fished the Hampshire Avon, which is so well suited to this style of fishing.

It was all done from the bank; long-trotting from a boat is childishly simple by comparison, especially when you can find a swim that allows you to run a float downstream without having to cast across the current. It is working across the current that complicates matters.

In most swims, the current is fastest in the middle of the river or thereabouts. That means that between you and the float there is slower water than that in which your float is running.

Straighten it

If you cast beyond the fastest water, it is even more complicated because your line is lying across water both faster and slower than that in which your float travels. In the first case, the line will travel slower than the float and form a curve; in the second case, some of it will go ahead of the float while some drags behind, and the line will form an S shape.

Wind, of course, adds still more difficulty!

Angling textbooks greatly over-simplify long-trotting. To read them, you might think that all the angler has to do is allow the float to draw line from the reel, while he brakes the latter gently, so as to check the float slightly and thus keep in touch with it. In practice, of course, he must be constantly picking the line off the water and laying it down straight. As soon as it bows or forms S-bends to any extent, it has to be picked off and straightened again.

Don't check

This has to be done without checking the progress of the float, more than can be helped, and, of course, without paying out more or less line than the float needs to allow it to travel along its chosen track. I find all this easier to do with a fixed-spool reel

21

than with a centre-pin. The centre-pin is fine for long-trotting straight down the current, but for cross-current work, give me the fixed-spool reel every time.

Proper control is made easier by the right choice of tackle. A float that grips the water helps a lot. The late Albert Smalley made splendid balsa-bodied floats with flutes in the sides, which go under easily when a fish bites, but aren't shifted out of their track when you straighten the line from rod tip to float.

Rod I used

It is very necessary to use a float that will carry enough weight. The swims I fished needed at least two swan-shot, and some of them three. I could find no advantage in spacing the shot; they were bunched, about 15in from the hook.

A long rod is of great advantage for long-trotting from the bank. For Avon roach and dace I've been using a four-piece ferruleless fibreglass rod, 13ft long, and it has behaved splendidly, catching chub up to 5$\frac{3}{4}$lb as well as dace and roach.

For big chub and barbel, however, I prefer something stouter. The best of my rods for this is a three-piece 14ft split-cane, but it is too heavy to use for more than two or three hours. If I expect to be trotting the same barbel swim all day, I use a 13ft rod in three joints that has a fibreglass butt and middle and a split-cane top.

Some of my long-trotting was done in the rain, which makes things more difficult. I wonder how many readers know the trick for knocking water off a rod? You give the rod a sharp blow with your left fist, just above where your right hand holds it—that is if you're a right-handed angler. The rod vibrates violently and throws most of the water off.

Don't do it with your float hanging just below the tip rings though, or you'll have a horrid tangle of float, shots, and hook wrapped round your top-joint.

Which reminds me—a little while ago I wrote about multipliers, and said that a small left-hand-wind multiplier with a gentle check would be fine for long-trotting. Ken Morritt, of Intrepids, pointed out that fishing with the rod-rings uppermost would be troublesome in the rain, and there's a lot in what he says. But then, long-trotting in the rain isn't easy at the best of times; I don't know which is worse, rain or wind!

New advantage

Whichever it is you have to contend with, more shot and a bigger float to carry them will help. I know we all like to keep float tackle as delicate as possible, but a heavy float that is under control all the time will get you far more fish than a light one that is being blown all over the place, or which refuses to draw line through wet rod-rings.

My recent experiences have left me in no doubt that the latest high-geared fixed-spool reels have great advantages for long-trotting. Before the advent of the roller guide in the pick-up, the combination of high gearing and high pick-up friction made rapid-recovery fixed-spool reels of doubtful advantage, but now we can benefit from the high gearing to recover the tackle for the next swim-down in much less time.

A final tip

One final tip, something I've mentioned before, but which can stand repeating: if you've had a bite and missed it, and the bait is still on, change it. In my recent fishing, I've been testing the value of this advice, and as a result I've become more than ever convinced of its soundness.

I don't say you'll never get a bite if you keep on fishing with a bait that's been in the mouth of a fish. I do say that you reduce your chance of a bite by ten times by carrying on fishing with such a bait, of course, I'm not counting bites from minnows or bleak; they'll take anything. Even if your crust or paste are untouched in appearance; even if your maggots or worms are unmarked and still wriggling; if you've had a definite bite on them and missed it, change them.

Fish are fastidious. They don't like food that somebody else has spat out.

5 Stret-pegging and laying-on

A young angler asked me last week, 'What's the difference between laying-on and stret-pegging?' He seemed to think I'd invented the term stret-pegging, incidentally, which isn't so. It is at least a hundred years old; but what its origin is, I don't profess to know.

Both laying-on and stret-pegging are methods of float-fishing in which the distance between the float and the hook is greater than the depth of the water. The difference is that in laying-on, the bait is anchored by the shot and left for the fish to find, whereas in stret-pegging, it is worked down the swim.

I expect I shall be asked what the difference is between laying-on and float-legering if I don't explain it now! Laying-on is done with shot or other lead *fixed* on the line; float-legering embodies a *running* lead, with the line passing through it or through a ring or loop attached to it, so that a biting fish doesn't have to move the lead to make the float register the bite.

Tackle-rigs for stret-pegging and laying-on aren't much different, though for the latter, I like a float that is long and slender and thus offers least resistance to the current, whereas for stret-pegging a shorter, fatter float is used. I don't mean an egg-shaped bob-float; the one I use is a modern equivalent of the old fashioned cork and porcupine Thames float, with a tapered body. My laying-on float is often one of Major Albert Smalley's 9in golden rod stems. Albert, in case you don't know, is the world's greatest float-maker and designer.

Stret-pegging demands skill born of practice. You cast downstream and hold up the tackle until it has straightened out. Then you lower the rod, which lets the shots rest on the bottom. Pause a while, then raise the rod again, draw a bit of line off the reel, then lower the rod. The shot, having been lifted, now comes to rest a little lower downstream. The float is lying tilted on the surface.

By repeating this process, the tackle can be worked a long way down a swim, the bait being on or close to the bottom all the time except when you lift it.

Sudden bites

You have to be very alert because many bites come as you're lifting, and with this method of fishing the bites are often quite sudden and violent. Not only does the float take a dive, but you may also get a bang on the rod top.

Of course there are other types of bite indication too. Sometimes the float lies completely flat instead of tilted; sometimes it moves across the stream, sometimes it just seems to sink slowly.

At first you may find it difficult to tell bites from float movements caused by the current, especially if the swim is rather turbulent, but experience teaches you to guess correctly most of the time, though you must expect to strike and miss quite often.

For stret-pegging at short ranges, especially when you're after roach, use a rod with a very flexible tip; and if you keep getting violent knocks and missing them, try putting either a swan-shot or an extra float on the line, above the float that is in the water. This acts as an extended dough-bobbin type of indicator, and prevents a biting fish feeling the resistance of the rod tip quite as quickly.

Stret-pegging is rather rough on baits, and while pastes and bread crust can be used, they come off the hook easily and you can waste a lot of time fishing with a baitless hook. I prefer to use either maggots or worms for the method. There are times when the water is high and coloured, but not muddy, and roach take worms freely. In these conditions, a little red cockspur worm on a No 12 round-bend hook will catch roach twice as fast as maggots, on many waters.

Of course, if you use big worms you must remember to drop a bit of slack when you see a bite, instead of striking at once. Wait till the float goes clear away before striking.

Change rods

When water conditions are such that stret-pegging is a method I expect to use, I like to have two or three rods with me, of various lengths, because the relationship of the rod length to the swim is quite important. I've found some swims that are best stret-pegged with a little eight-footer and others that needed a 14 or 15ft rod to fish them properly by this method.

The reason is that the float is always straight downstream

from the rod point, and you can't always adjust your seat at exactly the right distance from the bank.

Make no mistake, stret-pegging must be done along the right track in your swim; too close in or too far out are equally useless. Exactly what track you must fish depends upon the chosen swim and your judgement, and a lot of experimenting is often necessary. Don't give up a likely-looking swim until you've tried it at all distances from the bank, even if to do so means changing to a longer or a shorter rod to fish it properly.

I like to attach my float, which has no ring, by two pieces of rubber tube, so that I can change it easily. I can then change to a longer and thinner one, if my stret-pegging tells me that the fish are concentrated in one spot along the swim and that it would pay to lay-on in that spot instead of wasting time stret-pegging down to it.

Both stret-pegging and laying-on are good methodical ways of fishing, especially in winter. Learn to use them correctly, and you'll catch plenty of fish.

6 Finding fish even through the ice

We've had mild winters the past few years, so a little advice to anglers who haven't experienced a freezing spell like the one we had recently may help.

The important thing to remember is that a sudden fall in temperature puts nearly all fish right off feed. If the temperature stays low, the fish will start feeding again in a few days, but far less freely than they would in warmer water. They'll eat less, they'll take longer to digest what they do eat, and they'll be far less willing to move to find food, or to intercept moving baits. The critical temperature is, in my opinion, 39.2°F (fractionally under 4°C), and if the water is colder than that, you're unlikely to make a big catch.

Different values

This is where you've got to adopt a different set of values in your fishing. Success must be measured, not by the size of the catch, but by how your catch relates to the difficulties you encounter. The more you know about fish behaviour, the more you should enjoy your fishing, because you'll be as pleased to catch four or five roach of modest size, when the water is at, say, 37°F, as you would to catch thirty fish in water at, say, 48°F.

If you can't adapt your outlook in this way, you'd better go back home whenever you arrive at the water and find the temperature below that critical point of 39.2°F

Another thing to remember is that rising temperature gives you a better chance, even when the water is still well below 39.2°F, whereas falling temperature reduces your chances, even when the water is at 45°F or higher. Even so, it is difficult to catch fish in cold conditions compared to warmer ones. Because such conditions make fish less active, they usually move into slower water, or even slacks, in rivers, while in lakes or ponds they'll seek the deeper places. Small shallow ponds are unrewarding when the weather is cold, even when they're not frozen over.

Let the ice decide

When it is cold enough to freeze the surface of a river, it isn't difficult to decide where to fish, because the ice decides it for you. If you can find a place free from ice, then that is obviously a place where the water is a bit warmer than anywhere else, and that's where you can expect fish to be.

It always pays to look for the open space that has appeared naturally in ice, even if it means walking a long way, because such a place is far more likely to hold fish than a hole you've broken for yourself. Smashing ice doesn't exactly encourage fish to hang about, even if any were there in the first place.

Assuming you can find open water in a river, concentrate on fishing with an anchored small bait. Fish are unlikely to take trotted baits. So adopt legering or laying-on tactics, the second being the best choice if possible. Because fish don't move much in cold water, bites are liable to be very delicate, so the more sensitive indication given by float tackle is an advantage. I usually have something to say about touch legering being the

27

best way of detecting leger bites, but I certainly wouldn't advocate it in icy conditions; you won't feel bites with very cold fingers. So it's the float wherever possible.

Anchoring a bait doesn't mean chucking out, letting the tackle settle, and then waiting long periods for a bite. If you do that in cold water, unless your bait fetches up very close to a fish, you might wait for a bite all day. What you do is let your tackle settle, wait a minute or two, then move the bait six inches or so, wait a bit, then move it again; and keep on doing that till you find the fish. It's what is called 'scratching'.

You keep at it until you've covered carefully all the water within sensible casting distance; then you either cover it again, or try another swim. I said 'sensible casting distance' because this is no time for long-range fishing. To scratch properly, and detect small bite indications, it is better to work within 15 yards at most of where you're sitting.

Try crust or flake

Much the same applies to still waters, if you can find deep water close by. If not, you've no choice; you must get your bait in the deep places even if that involves a long throw and, probably, a proportion of undetected bites. First things first; you won't get any bites unless you put your bait where the fish are.

It is best to avoid excessive groundbaiting. Fish don't want much food in cold water, so it's all too easy to fill them up and put them off. All you need is a few hook-bait samples every quarter of an hour or so.

Except for perch, pike, and zander, you'll often find that small pieces of crust or flake will catch more fish than maggots do in cold water. It isn't of the slightest use warming maggots in your pocket to keep them wriggling actively, because the cold water will knock the wriggle out of them before they've sunk a couple of feet. If you want a good alternative to crust or flake, try small red worms, which will wriggle to some extent even in water near to freezing point.

Where you can reach really deep water, in lakes or reservoirs, you can use bigger baits, because the water in depths of 20ft or more seldom falls below about 42°F and fish will feed fairly freely in water at that temperature.

If you're fishing a lake that holds big perch, you can fish the biggest worms you can get in holes 20ft deep or more, with a good chance of success. This is where the angler who keeps a supply of worms in a big box scores. You won't find worms easy to get in freezing weather, in any other way. If you fish deep places of this sort, expect most bites when the light is brightest. If the sun comes out, your hopes should rise, but you may as well pack up directly the light begins to fail.

That applies pretty generally to fishing in very cold conditions, though there are exceptions to the rule, and if you're brave enough you may find roach starting to feed a little in the late afternoon, especially if it clouds over and the temperature stays up instead of falling as it more often does at that time of day.

It's important to take extra care when you go fishing in very cold weather and the three things to watch especially are dress warmly, have plenty of hot drinks, and don't fall in.

7 Big fish are not big fools

Since some doubts were expressed when I last wrote about concealment as to whether or not it is necessary, I would like to say a bit more about it now, because I think it is very important if you're after big fish.

I've been luckier than many anglers in that I've always lived near to waters that are very clear and where the fish can be seen fairly easily. Most of these waters are ones along whose banks the general public can and does walk. I say quite emphatically that where fish are regularly pursued by anglers, they remain suspicious of humans on the bank, no matter how often they may see them. The way in which they behave when their suspicions are aroused, either by seeing people or feeling the vibrations of a human tread, depends on the species of fish.

Most kinds of fish stop feeding at the first sign; if they are further scared, they bolt for cover. This applies especially to fish that go in shoals, and such fish are the least intelligent. They

29

have practically no reasoning powers and their reactions are simple.

More intelligent kinds of fish do become to some degree used to humans, including anglers, on the bank, and on very heavily fished waters sometimes continue feeding even when they know anglers are about. At such times they use their greater intelligence to discriminate, either between natural baits and baits commonly used by anglers, or between baits that have lines or floats attached to them and those which have not.

Chances spoiled

In saying that, I fully expect to be told that scientists have shown fish to be incapable of such feats of intelligence; if I am, my reply is that the scientists cannot have done much angling.

Irrespective of the circumstances in which you find your fish then, you always reduce, and usually completely spoil, your chances of catching them if you let them know you are there.

How can you best avoid letting them know it?

First of all, be careful how you tread. The two kinds of bank on which you need to take most care about this are the very hard bank and the very soft one. The hard bank rings if you tread heavily; the soft one quakes, and it is the worst of the two.

On some waters I fish it is next to impossible to reach the fish at all without scaring them by causing the bank to quake, and the only thing to do is to get into position and sit as quietly as possible until the fish have got over their scare. On any bank, you can't be too careful about treading not only as softly as possible, but as little as possible, too.

Fish see you

What about the fish seeing you?

When the surface of the water is calm, all the light that reaches the eyes of the fish comes through a circle above the fish's head. I don't intend to explain scientifically why this is so, but take it from me that it *is* so, and that this circle remains above the fish's head wherever it swims. It gets smaller the nearer to the surface the fish comes, and bigger if the fish goes deeper.

If you draw a line from the edge of this circle, 10° above the

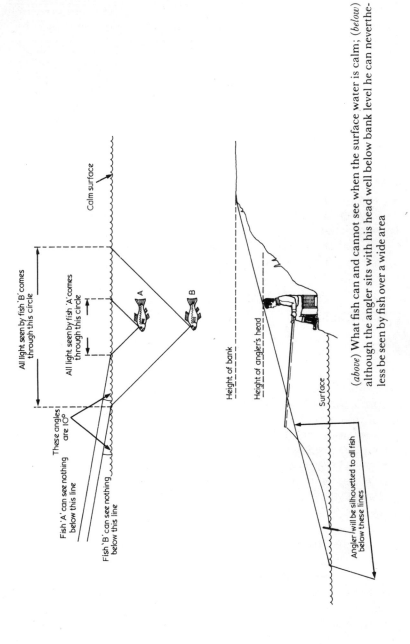

Calm surface

All light seen by fish 'B' comes through this circle

All light seen by fish 'A' comes through this circle

A

B

These angles are 10°

Fish 'A' can see nothing below this line

Fish 'B' can see nothing below this line

Height of bank

Height of angler's head

Surface

Angler will be silhouetted to all fish below these lines

(*above*) What fish can and cannot see when the surface water is calm; (*below*) although the angler sits with his head well below bank level he can nevertheless be seen by fish over a wide area

surface of the water and in any direction, that marks a limit below which the fish can see nothing, provided the surface of the water remains more or less unruffled. If you look at the top diagram you will see what I mean.

This means that if you, or part of you, comes above this 10° line, it is possible for the fish to see you. Whether the fish becomes aware of your presence then, depends on a number of things. You are much less likely to be seen if the bank behind you comes further above the 10° line than you do. If it does, and if you are dressed in garments of roughly similar colour to the bank and its vegetation, the fish is only likely to see you if the water is very clear. If it is clear, note that the deeper the fish is swimming, the easier it is for you to come above that 10° line.

When the water is to some extent coloured, you still may be spotted against a background of bank if you are wearing something, such as a white hat or shirt, that reflects much more light than the fish is accustomed to see coming from that particular direction.

Watch light

Now, let's have a look at what happens if you have not got a bank or something similar behind you when you come above the 10° line.

Most of the light that passes through the circle above the fish comes direct from the sky. The only other light coming through it is that reflected from such parts of the bank and surroundings as are above the 10° line, and these things absorb far more light than they reflect, so their contribution to the total that reaches the fish is very small.

If you shut off some of this reflected light by coming between part of the bank and the fish's circle, you won't make a great deal of difference to the total light, and that's why I said that under such circumstances the fish wouldn't be likely to notice you unless the water was fairly clear. But if you get directly between the sky—the main source of light—and the fish's circle, you will be shutting off a much greater proportion of the total light the fish sees, and whether the water is clear or as thick as can be, you are still shutting off the same proportion of all the light the fish gets.

Now, do you see that it follows from this that if you are silhouetted

32

against the sky, the only fish that won't be able to notice that you've shut off
some of his light is the fish that is either so deep, or in such dirty water, that
the light reaching him is less than his power of vision is able to detect?

Try it out

Let me tell you that there are very few waters that are as dirty or
as deep as all that!

All this applies when the surface of the water is reasonably
calm and flat. You may have noticed, in passing, that this
means that if you shine a light on the water, only that part of its
beam that strikes the surface at a steeper angle than 10° will
penetrate; the rest of the beam will be reflected off the surface
completely. You can try this out and see it for yourself.

When the surface is broken by ripples or waves, the whole
business of the 10° line is upset. Rays of light hitting the surface
at less than 10° are still reflected, of course, but the surface itself
is changing its angle all the time. What the fish can see becomes
indistinct, and broken up into momentary flashes. Perhaps
some idea of the effect can be obtained if I tell you it is much like
looking through the crinkled glass often found in lavatory win-
dows, only more as if the glass was constantly being moved
about.

Background

You know that if you look through glass of that kind you can see
no details at all, but if something comes between it and the
light, or a light object appears against a dark background, you
can spot it immediately.

So you'll see that when the surface is ripply, you can't get out
of sight of the fish by keeping below the 10° line as you could
when the surface is calm. You are less likely to be seen, when
the surface is ripply, if you harmonize more or less with the
background; but if you clash strongly with the background, the
rippled surface will not save you from being spotted, and may
even worsen your chances.

You could be wearing a white shirt and keeping below the 10°
line while the surface remained calm, and then be revealed to
the fish as a series of white flashes spread over quite a large
area, if a ripple is set up. Remember that it doesn't have to be a

continuous ripple or wave caused by wind. The rings caused by a rising or jumping fish, or your tackle being cast out, can do it too, as well as many other things that are always disturbing the surface.

And naturally, if you get between the fish and the sky, you are pretty sure to be spotted, ripple or no. You will still be coming between the fish and the main source of his light and *you will still be shutting off the same proportion of it.*

I hope by now that I have convinced you that it pays to wear sober-coloured clothes when you are fishing, and to take great care to *avoid being silhouetted against the sky, no matter how coloured the water may be, no matter how deep, and how broken its surface.*

Not easy

You may think that avoiding being silhouetted is easy. As a matter of fact, it's very difficult. You can easily think you've got a good background behind you when in fact you haven't.

You stand by the water's edge and look behind you, and you see the bank rising to a height well above your head. You think all is well. Now take a look at the bottom diagram (on page 31) and see how you can be wrong! A slope always looks a lot steeper than it really is. If you want to avoid being silhouetted, think of an imaginary string running between the top of the bank and a spot a yard nearer you than the place where the fish is—and keep well below that.

Does matter

Don't ever believe anyone who tells you that keeping out of sight of the fish doesn't matter. Many anglers fail to catch the big fish, much as they would like to do so. They often ascribe their failure to no big fish being there. In fact, they fail to catch them because they've scared the daylights out of them—in more ways than one.

Most of our rivers and lakes contain big fish, but those fish are not big fools.

8 Where there's weed there's big fish

Many angling clubs who have waters of their own ask me about weed cutting. Weed, they tell me, is their main problem. Having seen some of their waters I have come to the conclusion that many anglers will never be completely happy until they are able to fish in a swimming pool, complete with white tiles and deckchairs.

Of course, there are plenty of waters where a bit of weed cutting would do much to improve the fishing. There are also plenty where what is wanted is not less weed, but more. And there are a great many where indiscriminate weed cutting, and the removal of bankside vegetation is doing a great deal of harm.

Well known

I used to know half a dozen places on the Bedfordshire Ouse where I could nearly always catch a few chub, including a five-pounder now and then. They were places where there was a gravel bottom, kept scoured by the current because it ran between trailing weeds, or alongside beds of bulrush and was speeded up in consequence. On the banks were willow bushes whose branches trailed in the water. Against these branches would pile up little rafts of flotsam and jetsam, underneath which lived the chub.

At one time, I was always willing to tell fellow anglers whoever they were, all I knew about good spots to fish, and I told quite a few about these chub holes. The result was that they became quite well known.

Now, the majority of coarse fishermen have at least two things in common: reluctance to fish without a float, and belief that a 14 hook on 6x gut will land anything that swims, anywhere. Consequently, many who fished these chub holes lost hooks, floats, and some line by getting hung up on the willows and bulrushes. Many, too, smashed-up, now and then. But I didn't mind because all I lost was the No 6 eyed hook that was the only thing on my line, and cost about a penny. The other

35

chaps, however, had more expensive losses and they wanted to reduce them.

No chub now

So a wholesale clearance was effected. The willow branches were lopped, the weeds were cut, the bulrushes pulled out. Now the spots are much easier to fish, and you lose no tackle. You are never smashed-up now, because no chub remain to do the smashing. They've gone away.

Well, what else would you expect? If you discovered that the roof had been pulled off your house, the larder had been removed, and the floors covered with filth, would you continue to live in it?

Control of weed and bankside growths is often necessary, but it should be done to make better fishing. And better fishing doesn't necessarily mean easier fishing, nor does it mean greater ease of tackle manipulation, if that is being obtained at the expense of the fish. And far too often, it is.

When you think that almost the whole diet of fish springs in the first instance from plant growth, is it surprising that, generally speaking, it is from the weediest waters that the biggest fish come? If you want a specimen chub, the only river that I've fished that may yield a bigger one than the very weedy Hampshire Avon is the Wye, which is weedier still. I hear more complaints about the amount of weed in those two rivers than almost any other water, yet the big fish are there in quantity, in both rivers. And what's more, anglers who don't let weed scare them catch those big fish.

Weedy water

Knowing how to fish weedy water is part of the angler's art. I have spoken elsewhere about dealing with carp in weedy waters, but it isn't only a question of playing a hooked fish. There is also the question of choosing tackle, not only as regards its strength—and that must be adequate—but also the sort of rig to use.

There are many situations from which the majority of anglers would turn in disgust, saying they were unfishable, yet where good fish could be caught if the right methods were used.

36

Open swims

Remember, even on a water that has plenty of open, weed-free places, there will often be times when the fish are not in those easy, open swims, but among the oxygen-producing food-harbouring weeds.

If I've said it once I've said it a hundred times—if you want big fish you must fish where they are. You cannot catch a fish that isn't there. And if the fish are in weed, however thick, then in that weed you must fish, or fail. So don't be afraid to fish in it when it becomes necessary. You'll get hung up often, you'll get smashed-up often—but you'll get fish too.

9 Don't be fooled by those Fen drain fish

In *Angling Times* of 22 August 1963, Peter Tombleson's 'Information Corner' dealt with several subjects including fishing Fen drains.

I've done a good deal of fishing in waters of this kind, and I'd like to add a bit to what Peter said. Peter very rightly said that these drains offer very reliable fishing all the year round. They are subject to less temperature variation because their water comes from well under the surface of the soil.

But don't let the colour of water deceive you into thinking you can't be seen by the fish. If you dip out a glassful you'll find it is a lot clearer than it looks in the drain!

Many of these drains have flat banks—called 'the wash'—with a high bank or dyke between them and the surrounding fields. This dyke prevents an angler from being silhouetted against the sky, and if he is drably clad, the silt in the water will prevent fish from spotting him, since there is enough colour to make his outline very indistinct.

But let him dress up in a white shirt; or let the drain be one that has no dyke, and they'll spot him like a shot. So, although these drain waters are coloured, dress and move as though they were gin-clear.

Many of these drains are straight and featureless and it pays to put in time finding the fish. Feeding bream will produce extra colour in the water; tench will often send up their characteristic bubbles. In the smaller drains, you can often see the surface disturbed by fish moving near the bottom, because of the shallow water. Don't scorn the smaller drains, by the way, I've had big bream and tench from drains I could easily jump over.

Look for change

Another thing to look for, especially in very hot or very cold weather, is the outfall of a land drain. In summer it feeds in cool water; in winter, warmer water, and fish are likely to congregate around it.

In the absence of any other signs, look for anything that is an exception to the uniformity of a drain; a bend, a bush, even a different species of reed or rush in one place.

Peter Tombleson's suggestions about bait and groundbait are very sound, though on some drains, worm or maggots will produce unlimited quantities of 'bootlace' eels. So always have plenty of bread, so you can make paste or flake. *And don't forget that on some of these drains, stewed wheat can be deadly, especially if you can fish on three or four successive days and keep baiting up a swim.*

Watch out for predatory species—perch and pike. I've seen 4lb perch and 25lb pike taken from these little drains. If the bream and roach won't oblige, try a big worm on paternoster tackle, with a couple of swan-shot instead of pear lead, so as to reduce the splash when you cast. Make a long throw up or down the drain and work the tackle back very slowly; if you get a pull, slack off, count ten, and strike.

Some drains hold lots of perch, others very few. If you find one of the former, you can have fine sport spinning with a little vibrating spoon, or you can take a can of minnows and fish them on float-tackle. I had twenty perch once, using minnows and an oak-apple for a float; all between 1 and 2lb, from a drain near Ely.

As for the pike, you could encounter a record fish in these waters. In the autumn, big pike start moving into the smaller waters, and by Christmas, it isn't uncommon to find big ones in ditches so narrow that they have to do a three point turn to face the other way.

In the old days, more than one thirty-pounder left a narrow Fen drain at the end of a long-handled pitchfork, or floated up flapping with a charge of shot from a twelve-bore in the back of its head.

Like a rocket

No special methods of pike fishing are needed, but do remember that a whopper hooked in a narrow water, is likely to take off like a rocket. Make sure that all is clear to give line, before you strike; and don't sit glued to your stool or basket. Keep level with the fish as far as possible, so you can stop him from jamming his head into the reeds on either side.

One more kind of fish that it is just possible you may meet if you fish these drains often, is an enormous eel. I don't mean a mere four or five-pounder, but something well into double figures. These chaps are few and far between, but they do exist—up to 20lb or more.

Nobody, as far as I know, has ever caught one on rod and line, but they've been seen many times, and occasionally shot, snared, or speared. If you spot one, you might just have a faint chance of landing it on stout pike tackle, after which the reel fight would just be starting!

Ask a farmer

Although more and more Fen waters are being rented by clubs and associations, there are miles and miles of drain that anyone can fish, provided he asks permission from the farmer. *I would add that many farmers like to eat pike, perch and eels, and those who don't will still appreciate the offer.*

Perhaps the main reason why so few of the big pike that inhabit Fenland are caught is the east wind. In winter it seems to blow on four days out of five, and it is really daunting.

If you fish the Fens then, you'll need the warmest clothes you've got; it's like being in Iceland, only worse. They haven't seen a brass monkey there for centuries.

10 Night fishing hints

During July and August I receive many letters asking for advice about night fishing and the use of electrical bite alarms. Perhaps I can save some readers the trouble of writing if I answer their queries now!

The most important thing about night fishing is making yourself comfortable. You need a really comfortable seat with a back-rest. It shouldn't be too high because the nearer you are to the ground the better you can see, after dark. If you can manage it, use a deckchair; if that is impracticable, use a small folding chair, or make yourself a special seat. Ordinary baskets and stools just won't do.

Clothing is equally important. It can be really cold on a summer night, so wrap yourself up accordingly. This is important. If you're cold and uncomfortable, you tend to move about more and scare fish. You're at your chilliest and stiffest just at dawn, when the bite from that monster fish is most likely to come. If you're not at your best, you may miss it.

Take plenty of hot drinks, in flasks. Don't go stumping up the bank to light a stove and brew up with your friends at 2 am. Have everything set out so that you do the absolute minimum of moving about. I've seen night fishing parties recently that were not only wrecking their own chances of fish but everyone else's too. One lot found it necessary to brew up tea or coffee about every two hours. First a big Tilley lamp was lit that illuminated the countryside for about a hundred yards around. Then after a few minutes came a yell of 'Come and get it!' Whereupon four or five people at different spots round the lake switched on their torches and marched towards the big light. A radio was turned on full blast to entertain the party while they consumed their drinks, which took about three-quarters of an hour.

Needless to say nobody caught anything, and I imagine local residents must have been pretty sore about the whole business. No wonder many clubs and associations bar night fishing. Their attitude is understandable, if not entirely logical; for what they really should ban is this stupid behaviour, not fishing at night.

The whole point about fishing at night is that everything is, or should be, quiet and peaceful. If you can't keep it that way you might as well go home. If you yearn for bright lights and music, why not try the local dance-hall?

So much for peace and quiet. What about choice of pitch?

Choose your spot in daylight. Keep clear of overhanging branches or bankside bushes, if you possibly can. You'll probably be using groundbait; if so, you must be sure you can put it and your baited hook in the right place. So line up marks on the skyline opposite.

Tag your casting distance with a marker on your line, if you're legering, so that you can cast over, in the dark, and then wind back until you can feel the marker.

One form of night fishing involves using a light shining on the float. If you do this, be sure your light is as near the surface of the water as possible, so that it shines across the water, not down into it. Keep it fixed; don't move it about. A low lamp with its beam parallel to the surface of the water, kept still, doesn't seem to scare fish, but a light that keeps flashing about, or which is pointed downwards, most certainly will. There may still be some anglers who believe that lights attract fish, so I'd better add that while some kinds of sea fish may be attracted, our ordinary freshwater coarse fish aren't. On the contrary, lights can scare them badly.

Many readers are puzzled about setting electric bite alarms. I fancy their puzzlement may arise from illustrations that have been published showing rods in bite alarm rests with the butt ring in front of the vee of the rest. With the reel pickup open, no antenna type alarm can work with the rod set so. The correct way to put the rod in the rest is with its butt ring or even the second ring, behind the antenna. This causes the line to be out of straight where it passes round the antenna. When a bite comes, the friction at the rod-rings is enough to cause the line to try to straighten, thus moving over the antenna and sounding the alarm.

It takes a little experimenting to learn just where to lay the rod to bring its rings in the best position for reliable operation, but once you've found it you'll have no more difficulty.

When carp fishing, I think it is best to flick a couple of feet, or more, of slack, on to the water before setting the rod in its rest and adjusting the bite alarm. Then a biting carp can move at least that far before feeling any resistance whatever.

Don't run away with the idea that fishing at night is the answer to all your big-fish-catching problems. On the contrary, night fishing means overcoming quite a lot of difficulties and learning new methods.

If you do catch a big fish in the dark, you'll deserve it.

11 There's more to legering than just waiting

I continue to get a lot of letters asking for more information about legering. It seems that quite a lot of anglers have only recently found out that there's more in it than just casting out and waiting for a bite. Some seem to think that they've only to change from float-fishing to legering to catch bigger fish, but it isn't quite as simple as that.

I think it is a mistake to adopt any angling method for its own sake or because others have done well with it. There is no best all-round method of catching fish, big or little, and if you stick to only one method, it will be the wrong method more often than not, except perhaps when you're after the same kind of fish all the time in conditions that don't vary very much.

Legering is often an effective way of fishing, though, so I'll try to deal with some of the finer points in it. First of all there's the matter of the stop-shot which prevents the lead from sliding down to the hook. I've been asked how far this should be from the hook.

Shot distances

That depends on the kind of water you're fishing and what sort of fish you're after, and sometimes, too, on the bait and the way the fish are feeding. For example, there are times when tench and big roach can be taken on a small crust, a grain of wheat, or a very small red worm, when they wouldn't look at a big bait, and at such times they won't hang on to even a small bait very long.

At such times—which are not very common, but have to be met when they occur—it is best to put the stop-shot very close to the hook, only a couple of inches or so, and then you get an indication of a bite much sooner than you would if you had a yard between hook and lead. When stillwater roach and tench, are feeding well, however, it's best to have 3ft or so between hook and lead, so that the fish don't brush against the line between lead and rod, or move it with the wash from their fins and tails.

A mouthful

This extra length beyond the lead also gives a fish a chance to get the bait well into its mouth before it feels any drag, and in general it's advisable for any fish unless other considerations decide you against it.

Besides the case I mentioned about roach and tench, there are other times when a short distance between lead and shot is best. If you're fishing in very fast water with a bait like crust or lobworm that tends to lift in the current, you will have to keep it close to your lead if you want it close to the bottom, especially if your swim is where two currents converge and make the water eddy upwards.

If your quarry is barbel, or winter chub or roach, for example, you will want to keep the bait well down; but in summer when you're after chub, you may want it to rise a bit, so you must increase the distance between lead and hook to let it.

A short distance between lead and hook is also used in one of the ways of fishing over a silkweed-covered bottom, for carp and tench especially. Crust is used for bait, which tends to float; so if you set the distance between hook and lead about equal to the depth of the silkweed, and draw the line tight after casting out, your crust will appear to the fish to be resting on top of the silkweed, and they won't see much else, because your lead and some of your line will be hidden in the weed. This is a useful way of legering at times and I caught my first carp over 20lb using it.

Remember, though, that in stillwater fishing you can often manage without a lead at all, and it usually pays to do so if circumstances allow it.

With the fish tightly shoaled behind the rush bed, both float-fished and legered baits must be held tight to keep them in position. The tighter the line between rod tip and bait, the quicker the biting fish will feel resistance

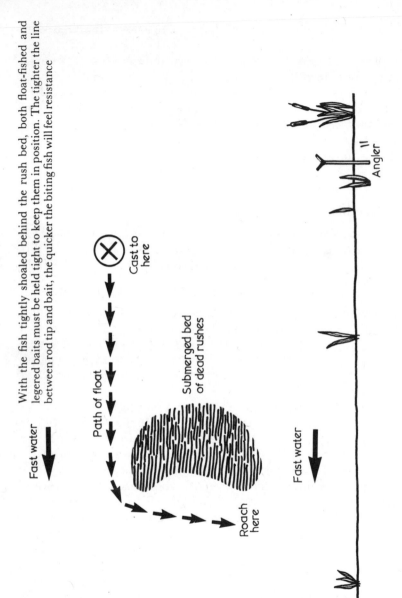

Fast water

Path of float

Cast to here

Submerged bed of dead rushes

Roach here

Fast water

Angler

I've also been asked about whether there should be a shot above the lead as well as below it. There may be a good reason why a lot of people put this second shot on, but I can't see what it is, except on rare occasions when your bait is a good deal heavier than the lead. Then, the bait is liable to draw a lot of line through the lead as it flies out when you cast, which ruins accuracy. A shot above the lead stops this; but it also limits the distance a fish can go before it has to drag the lead.

Avoid drag

This doesn't matter so much in running water, where you will have struck before a fish has gone far; but it is usually fatal when you're after big perch or carp in still water. These fish generally go several yards before taking the bait in properly and they'll spit it out quick if they feel any drag.

It's been suggested that this shot above the lead causes a fish to hook itself when it comes up against the drag, but while that may happen once in a while, I wouldn't mind betting that far more fish drop the bait because of it than ever hook themselves.

So much for the matter of the shot. Now there is the business of casting. Some chaps seem to think that any old wreck of a rod with a cut-down top will do for legering. Actually, a rod that has got to cast a leger far and accurately needs to be as carefully designed and well made as any rod in existence. If it's too stiff, it will force you to use a lead to suit the rod instead of the water conditions, which means too heavy a lead. It will also make you use too strong a line to avoid breakage, not only in casting that too-heavy lead, but also on the strike. If the rod is too whippy it will be strained in casting and be too soft to move the lead on the strike properly.

The way you cast is your own affair; I've got pretty definite ideas on that, but they'd take too long to expound here, beyond saying that if you're doing the work instead of the rod there's something wrong.

Several river anglers that have tried legering for the big ones for the first time tell me they've broken at the strike more than once even using flexible rods. Well, anyone that says he's never broken at the strike when legering has either not done much, or else he's done it wrong, or else he's a liar. Even anglers that do more legering than anything else, and have been doing it for

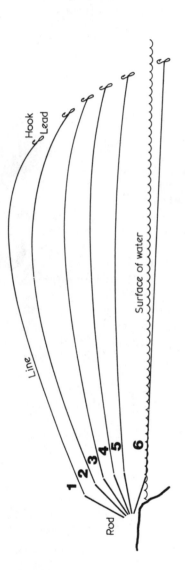

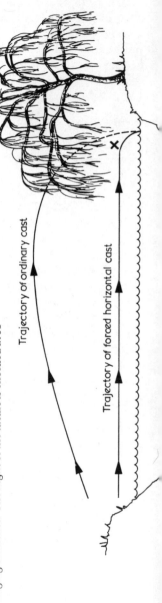

(*above*) Six stages in the straightening-out process when casting to beat the wind. The line is checked at 1, straightens out at 2,3,4 and 5 and cuts below the surface at 6; (*below*) how the forced horizontal cast gets a leger under over-hanging branches. The flight of the tackle is checked at X

years and years, break at the strike now and then. Even a small chub of 3lb or so can give a terrific tug and on a leger you get it direct. If you've not had a bite for some time it's apt to catch you unawares, and you strike much too hard and lose the lot.

But to a chap who's always been a float-fisher till then, the first good bite or two he gets on leger must feel like the kick of a mule, and he must expect a few smashes until he gets the feel of the thing. He can reduce their number by commencing his legering with tackle at least twice as strong as he would have chosen for float-fishing, and by not only using a bendy rod but striking from the reel always.

Remember, though, that the bite isn't always violent. Sometimes there's just a sensation as if the rod point were getting heavier. Strike! Sometimes everything suddenly goes slack. Strike! Sometimes there's a sort of vibration as if the line were being rubbed with a coarse file. Strike at that too.

But I hope, when you leger, you'll get your fair share of those tremendous thuds that nearly take the rod out of your hand and make you wonder, if you have time to wonder, whether it's a fish or a submarine.

They're among the most exciting things in angling.

12 Difficult bites on leger tackle

Fred Taylor has described the difficulty he and others have experienced in hitting the bites they get from Ouse roach when they are legering.

Although I fish the same stretch of river with Fred, I have done very little legering for roach, and I don't imagine that I should do any better at striking these tricky bites than Fred, or Peter Stone, who is probably the most skilled exponent of legering for roach that I am ever likely to see.

Deepest holes

But I do catch a great many roach from this water, most of them by float-fishing and some of them by accident when legering for chub. Nearly all of the latter are fish that I think hook themselves, and it has been while I have been float-fishing that I have had a number of bites that may give some clue to the problem.

At the back-end of the coarse fishing season, the upper Ouse often runs very clear and, without being specially high, quite fast.

The roach, most of which have spent the depth of the winter in the deepest holes, the clay-bottomed places where the lilies grow in summer, move at this time into shallower, gravel-bottomed places, but because of the current speed they seek some shelter. This they find in the form of beds of rushes. The rushes are, of course, dead; but the dead stalks remain in big clumps below the surface, and the current passing through these clumps is considerably slowed, and some of its turbulences are smoothed out. The result is an area of smooth, slower water downstream of the rush-clump and it is into this that the roach move.

One cannot swim float tackle down to these fish in a straight line, because it gets hung up on the dead rushes. Nor is it of any use to cast the tackle to alight directly below the rush-bed, because the current quickly whips it too far below before the baited hook can sink sufficiently deep.

The only way in which I can succeed is to cast across stream, beyond the rush-clump, allow the tackle to run down the current on the far side, and, at the critical moment, check it and allow it to swing into the slacker water. By then paying out a couple of feet of line, the bait can be manoeuvred into the right place. It cannot be kept there long; either it must be allowed to go downstream, or, if again checked, it swings inwards and ends up trailing downstream directly in line with the rod point.

Steady stream

Ordinarily, the roach are concentrated in a pretty tight bunch, close below the rush-clump; but by putting in a steady stream of maggots upstream of the place, the roach can be made to spread out somewhat and the area in which bites can be expected is extended.

48

This brings me to the interesting thing; when the tackle is swinging, either into or out of the slacker patch, there often comes a bite. Presumably a roach, encouraged by the maggots coming loose down the current, has made a grab at the bait as it swings. The line is at that time nearly, if not quite, taut from bait to rod point, and the bite is fast and violent. Not only does the float move; there is a violent 'jag' on the rod point.

Only the most rapid response results in a hooked fish and I miss nine out of ten of these bites. They are in direct contrast to the type of bite I get while the float is dwelling (for want of a better term) in the slow water, not swinging, and with a foot or two of slack between rod tip and float. The bites I get then are firm, decisive, and not particularly fast. The float dips and then either swings downstream or glides across the current. Very occasionally it moves up towards the rushes.

One can very easily visualize what the fish has done, and there seems little doubt that the bait has been taken and held with the greatest confidence. I hardly ever miss these bites. This seems to be evidence that the type of bite received is dependent upon the tackle and the way it is fished and not some idiosyncrasy on the part of the fish.

The bites that are hard to hit are those in which the line is drawn taut to the rod top. I am sure the fish feel the resistance of the rod top and eject the bait quicker than the angler can strike, in the majority of cases.

When the bait is swinging round, its progress is intermittent, because the distance between float and lead (usually one large swan-shot) exceeds the depth of the water, and irregularities in the bottom check the lead, which stops, then rolls as the current swings the float, then perhaps swings temporarily clear of the bottom.

The lightning 'jag' bites are produced by biting fish that move down, or down and across the current. But I have not infrequently retrieved at the end of the swing round only to find a fish is on. This, I surmise, is a fish that after taking the bait, moved up or up and across the stream. This could hardly happen with a properly arranged leger tackle having an easily running lead, because whichever way the fish moved, it would come up against the resistance, either of the lead or the rod tip or both. So legering downstream for roach can hardly fail to produce these quick, unhittable bites, if done at short range.

49

Good catches

The shorter the range, the less the distance the fish can move before feeling the resistance of the rod tip, and that is not the whole story.

It isn't only the matter of the fish coming up against this resistance; it is how it encounters it. On a short line, it will do so abruptly. On a long line, the resistance the biting fish feels will increase much more progressively and smoothly.

I have had good catches of roach on leger tackle in circumstances where the use of leger tackle was dictated largely by the range at which I had to fish. I remember specially a good number of large roach I caught in the House Pool on the Royalty Fishery, using a 5lb line, a No 10 hook, if memory serves correctly, and a 1oz Arlesey bomb. It is true that bite indications were delicate and that I missed some but the proportion of misses was not too high.

Heavy lead

Now those roach evidently didn't mind a heavy lead, a thick line by roach fishing standards, or a big hook by the same standards. And before they could feel the rod, they had to straighten out a bow in the line caused by 40yd of intervening heavy current, the direction I was casting being down and across.

By holding the line between butt ring and reel I could feel the line begin to tighten and strike accordingly. There was no 'jag' on the rod tip, nor could there be except from the most violent pull from a fish because of the cushioning effect of the line between rod and fish.

This may account for the fact that Fred Taylor and Peter Stone found it much easier to hook roach on leger tackle in the Thames than in the Ouse. On the Thames, they fish at very much greater range, and because the depth is greater, more of their line is in the water even at shorter range. There is more cushion effect.

Next season, I shall try legering for the Ouse roach with a couple of rod rests arranged so that my rod points straight down the line at the leger lead. I shall have a dough-bobbin-like device to clip on the line between butt ring and reel, that can be loaded so that it just balances the effect of the current on that

50

part of the line that is in the water. I shall sit with my hand on the rod butt, ready to strike directly that device starts to move up. Whether it will solve the problem remains to be seen!

13 Timing the strike is vital when legering

I am still being asked questions by readers about legering. The thing that puzzles many is the timing of the strike. It seems that a lot of anglers still think that legering is simply a matter of casting out a lead heavy enough to hold bottom, then putting the rod in a rest and waiting for a bite.

Of course, there are some kinds of fishing where that is the right thing to do. Carp, perch, tench, and eels are all fish that, as a rule, give you plenty of time to strike, and provided you arrange things so that you can strike before the fish feels a check, you can afford to allow up to several seconds. It may even be necessary to allow time for a fish to get the bait well into its mouth, as when using a big worm for perch or tench, or a dead fish for eels.

Rod in rest

In all these kinds of fishing, the rod can be in a rest, and you should make provision for the biting fish to take as much time as you think is necessary before he pulls it tight. You mustn't expect those kinds of fish to hold on to a bait after they've pulled the rod top down and felt the check of it.

For most other kinds of fish, however, and even for perch in fast water, you need to strike quickly as soon as you feel or see a bite. For that reason it is necessary to hold your rod all the time, even when you are keeping your leger in one place.

Roach and dace very often eject a bait almost immediately

after taking it, even when they feel no check. This is specially obvious in heavily fished waters, even still ones. Perhaps they are quick to feel the hook.

Quick water

In quick water, most kinds of fish are apt to eject a bait more quickly maybe because they feel the pull of the current on the line even before they get much of a pull on the rod. The extent to which they do this depends to some degree on the size of the fish. *The smaller the bait and fish, the quicker you must strike.*

In my experience, when legering in rivers having anything more than a very gentle flow, it definitely pays to hold the rod all the time, with the line tight to the rod top. No dough-bobbins or anything of that kind, if you can help it. You'll either see the knocks on the rod tip, or feel them. What you do then depends on what kind of fish you're expecting and what bait you're using.

With small baits, such as wheat, hemp, pearl, barley, maggots (whether one, two, or three on a hook), small worms, flake, or small pieces of bread or cheese paste, I usually try to hit them 'on the bounce',—that is, as soon as I see or feel the knock I strike smartly in the opposite direction—provided I get a knock.

But you don't, always. Sometimes you get a sort of trembling feeling in the line, and then I think it is best to ease ever so slightly to the fish waiting for a more decisive pull.

With bigger baits, I often find it necessary to strike experimentally at first, at everything that is sure evidence of a fish at the bait. If I fail to connect I try waiting for more definite bites but often such delay means missed chances. You see, you're never sure at first what is responsible for light touches. It may be small fish, and if it is, it's no good striking at everything, because you'll be losing bait and scaring fish, and you'll spend nine-tenths of the day with your hook out of the water.

You must wait for the better fish. When small fish are about and a big one comes along and takes your bait, you generally get a good solid bite from it. But sometimes you can be fishing where there are few small fish, but plenty of bigger ones, which latter may bite delicately, refusing to give you a good pull. Quick striking may hook some of these.

52

Experience alone teaches you the difference between the bite that is indecisive because the biter is small, and the nibble of a big fish, and it will also teach you when to strike smartly at the latter, and when to wait a bit. All I can tell you is to try and translate the movement of the line, or rod tip, into a message about what the fish is doing with your bait, and act accordingly.

You learn

Trial and error will teach you much. For example, if you're fishing with a big worm and find after striking at a bite that half the worm has gone, you will naturally give the next biter a bit more time and a few inches of slack line.

To save your arm, you can let a rod rest carry the weight of the rod, still holding the butt ready to strike—but make sure it is a rest from which rod and line can come away clear every time you strike.

Test first

And always strike from the reel, never grasp the line against the rod butt or hold it in your spare hand. Set your reel so that when you strike, it will neither yield line too easily and perhaps over-run, nor be so stiff that you break, however hard you may strike.

Don't find out you were wrong with the help of a fish—test it before you begin.

14 Don't be a soft touch, bend that rod after striking

Nowadays the angler who wants to leger has a wide choice of rod tips that act as bite indicators and at the same time fulfil another function that is not so well understood. We have swing tips, spring tips, quiver tips, and hinged tips. All these devices, as well as indicating bites, also serve to reduce the effects of a biting fish feeling the rod top.

A good many years ago, the Taylor brothers, Peter Stone, and I used to puzzle our heads over the problems of catching roach on leger tackle, specially in the Upper Great Ouse. This stretch of the river is narrow and the fishing mostly had to be done at short range.

Distance

We missed about 95 per cent of the bites, using ordinary rods with normal tops. On other rivers, like the Thames and the Hampshire Avon, we missed a very much smaller percentage of bites. After a lot of thought and discussion, we came to the conclusion that the answer was to be found in the distance at which we fished.

At the longer ranges on the bigger rivers, there was a good sized curve in the line between rod top and bait, which in being partly straightened out by a biting fish, acted as a cushion. At short ranges, there was far less cushioning effect, which meant the fish felt the rod top much more readily and were able to spit the bait out before we could strike.

Where the nature of the Ouse swims allowed it, we then tried fishing at longer range and found that we hit more bites, though the number of misses was still too high. We tried experiments with air floats and bobbins on the line beyond the rod tip, and these helped.

Nowadays, of course, I'd use a spring or quiver tip for the same kind of fishing, and even for longer range work in slow or still water where there was little or no current to put a bow in the line.

Having learned something of the art of touch-legering, I don't need special tips to act as bite indicators, but they do have this other use, of cushioning the bite and causing a biting fish to hang on just that bit longer, long enough for the strike to take effect.

It is important to remember, though, that anything that cushions the bite must inevitably cushion the strike. The combination of fibreglass rods and nylon lines has already made it more difficult to drive hooks home. Where small hooks, from 12 to 20, are used, the trouble isn't too serious, though one still reads report after report in which losses of fish by matchmen are reported.

These losses are hardly ever due to breakage. They are almost always caused by hook-hold failure. Failure of the hook-hold is sometimes the result of using very small hooks, which only hold the fish by a fragile bit of skin. If that gives way, the fish is lost. I think it is likely, however, that at least as many fish are lost because the hook was never driven properly home, and that the cause was too much cushioning of the strike by the combined effects of stretchy nylon line, lightweight glass rod, and bite indicating tip.

Resistance

If driving home hooks properly is a problem with smallish hooks, it is a far greater one with comparatively large hooks, size 10 to 2. In fact, I don't think that these larger hooks can really be struck home at all. What we have to do is pull them home, as soon as possible after the point has been started on its way in.

What you do is strike in the ordinary way and then, as soon as you feel the fish, bend the rod quite hard against the resistance of that fish, and keep it so bent as long as you think wise. If you overdo it, of course there is a risk that a big fish will do something violent and break you. So it is a matter of skill and judgement to get it right. Fortunately, big fish usually stay inert for an appreciable time after being struck; long enough to allow you to pull the hook home before they 'take-off'.

It is surprising how much pull you can apply to a line without risk of breakage. Just try tying your line to a post or tree, 15 to 20yd away, and seeing how much you can bend your rod before the line breaks.

This technique also helps to overcome another difficulty you sometimes encounter when legering in fast water, especially when you have quite a lot of line across the current and are using a fairly heavy lead or string of shot to hold position.

Dislodged

With the tackle so arranged, you have a steady pull on the lead acting mainly in a downstream direction, because although the lead may be on the bottom at a point almost directly across stream, the line is in a curve, so that it comes away from the lead in a downstream direction.

All this pull on the lead means that only a small extra pull is needed to shift it. When a fish bites, the lead is dislodged, and the current takes hold of it, washing it several feet downstream. At the same time, the angler gets a bite indication. His following strike has to straighten out a sharp angle between him and the fish, with the lead at the corner of the angle. Here again you can try an experiment to see how much effect this has. Tie the end of your line to a spring balance which is in turn attached to some convenient fixed point.

Absorbed

Attach a 1oz lead to the line, 4 or 5ft from the balance. Now lay this lead on the ground with the line to the balance taut, and walk away at right angles to that bit of line. Get a friend to watch the spring balance when you strike. What he sees will confirm that nearly all the power of your strike is absorbed in moving the lead. The pull on the balance is quite tiny. It'll be even less when it happens under water, because of the water drag on line and lead.

So here again, it pays to bend the rod hard against any fish you hook, immediately after striking. If you do that, you'll have far fewer of those brief encounters, in which you feel a fish momentarily and then the line goes slack.

15 Choose a bait that fish can smell

Rising water usually means coloured water, and coloured water needs thinking about if you are to catch fish from it.

The most common fallacy about coloured water is that it removes the need for concealment. It doesn't. Next time you find a river in flood, running dirty brown and looking as if you couldn't see an inch through it, just dip out a glassful. It isn't nearly as coloured as you thought, is it?

Water has got to be very, very strongly coloured indeed before no light can get through it at all. If any light does get through the fish can tell if you shut some of it off—if you get between them and the sky.

Winter flood

It's just as important to avoid coming between the water and the sky when the river is in winter flood as when it is gin-clear and low water in summer.

Although fish can tell, in dirty water, if something has come between them and the light, they can't distinguish objects far, and the chub, that might have come several yards after your bait in clear water, because he could see it, will need the bait much nearer, in dirty water, before he'll find it by sight. The same applies to other fish.

Fortunately, they have another way of finding food. They detect its flavour in the water. Let's say they smell it. For that reason, it's a good idea, when the river is running dirty, to use a bait that fish can smell easily. Cheese paste is one bait of that sort. A lobworm is another. I know lobworms don't smell very much to you. If they do it's time they were thrown away. But even the freshest lobworms smell strongly to fish.

Anyone who has some perch in a garden pond or aquarium can prove that. Just pour in a few drops of water that lobs have been washed in and see the perch dash about looking for the worms that aren't there.

Everyone knows the value of a lob in coloured water, of course. Not only can fish scent it, but the soil that produces the colour has been washed off the banks, and worms have been washed away too, which the fish are expecting.

Although fish can still detect an angler on the bank when the water is muddy the angler cannot detect them and nor can their other enemies. They know this, and when the water is thick they will often venture into very shallow water, where they would seldom dare to go when the water was clear, except at night when the sky is cloudy. I've caught roach, dace, bream, tench, and chub in water that hardly covers their backs, when the water has been muddy and the weather not too chilly.

Shallow water

On mild winter days it pays to watch out for fish movement in very shallow water. Often a tell-tale swirl can be spotted, and a fat worm cast near it may produce a hefty chub or roach, or a dace or barbel.

Coloured water seems to affect the preferences of roach and dace. The crafty old roach that won't look at anything bigger than a maggot on a No 16 in clear water, will grab a whole lob on a No 6 when the water is running thick. Pike and perch can detect the vibrations made by the smaller fish on which they prey, and when they can't see very well they depend on this ability to get their food.

If you're spinning in coloured water, you want a lure that works slowly, kicks up considerable disturbance and has plenty of flash.

It is always important, if you use groundbait, to know where it has found bottom, but never more important than when the water is dirty.

Swim-feeder

In clear water, your hook bait can be some distance from the groundbait, and will be seen and taken by an odd fish or two. In coloured water, it must be right among the groundbait, and if you can't be dead sure of that, it is better to use no groundbait at all. There's a great deal to be said in favour of using a swim-feeder in such conditions, especially when after roach and dace.

What I find exciting about fishing a coloured water—one that has colour because of rain or flood water—is that one never knows what the next bite may produce.

Fish stouter

Fish move all over the place in such conditions, and the next pluck on the leger or dip of the float may mean anything from a gudgeon to a really big barbel or chub. For that reason it pays to fish a pound or two stouter than usual. You don't want to smash in that whopper when he grabs your bait.

16 Where to find fish in cold weather

In very cold conditions, most kinds of fish are hard to catch. It is then that the thoughtful angler who realizes that such conditions require special tactics will succeed when others fail. Let's consider some general points about cold weather fishing.

Lots of anglers shun still waters in winter, but actually such waters often fish well until complete icing-over makes angling impossible. The great point about such waters is that once the water temperature has got below 39°F, it becomes much easier to find where the fish are.

Water becomes heavier and heavier the more it is cooled, until its temperature is about 39°F. In a lake, that means that at temperatures above 39°F, the warmest water is at the top. But once the temperature gets below 39°F, water begins to get lighter again; which is why ice floats. Once the water has fallen below 39°F, the warmest water will be at the bottom.

The only exception to this rule for still waters is where they are fed by streams. If the stream is bringing in land drainage its water may be warmer than that in the lake, and if so it will attract fish. Your thermometer will tell you if this is likely.

Simple rules

So you have quite a simple set of rules for lakes, ponds, pits, reservoirs, etc. If the temperature is over 39°F, the fish—that is such fish as remain active in winter—may be in the shallows, especially if the temperature has risen recently. If the temperature is below 39°F and there is no feeder stream bringing in warmer water, expect to find your fish in the deepest parts of the lake.

In rivers, things are different. The current is constantly rolling the water over and over and mixing it, and most anglers have seen ice covering the bottom as well as the top.

But cold conditions have the same effect on fish in both still and running waters in one respect—they make the fish less active. That means that in rivers you may expect to find the fish moving into slacker water as the temperature falls. It also means that in cold conditions fish will be less inclined to move about in search of food, and you must make your bait easy for them to get.

When it is really cold you can often catch fish on a rolling leger that you'd never have touched by swimming a bait down on float-tackle, especially if you cover the water very slowly and methodically, letting your bait hang for minutes at a time in the likeliest places.

If you get a bite in a given spot, then concentrate on that exact spot as hard as you can, for fish tend to bunch together in cold conditions and where one is, there are probably a lot more.

Sluggish

Don't forget how sluggish most species are at such times. You must try to hang your bait right over their very noses, and if you can do that, you'll probably find a fish willing to move itself a few inches to take your bait, when it has had a look at it for long enough. A bait coming down with the current would have passed by long before the fish's dulled intelligence had awakened to the fact that food was about.

Much the same applies in still waters, and your bait should be left to be on the bottom much longer than would be normal for summer and autumn conditions, except in the case of rather specialized kinds of fishing, like carp. Groundbait can help, but it wants to be of a kind that will go right where the fish are and stay there.

Take chub fishing, for example. In summer you can use a groundbait that rolls down with the current and keep putting it in. You can attract chub from a long way then, but in winter you want something more solid, and if it is really cold, something that goes down like lead, dead in the spot where the fish already are, and stays there, so they can have lots of time to make up their minds that food is there which won't need a lot of effort to get.

Simple way

I am sure readers will have noticed that quite a lot of pike, and big ones too, have been caught lately in what seems to be about the simplest way one could imagine. I expect most anglers thought, as I did, that it needed a moving bait to attract pike.

About a year ago, Fred Taylor, of Aylesbury, told me that he had been catching plenty of pike with a dead bait lying still on the bottom.

Dead bait

Mr A E Neale, of Hertford, one of the most knowledgeable anglers I ever met, told me that whenever he wanted to get rid of a big pike that was proving a nuisance in his trout preserves, he used a dead fish, often a good-sized herring, and let it lie on the bottom, close in to the bank and preferably near reeds or rushes, until the pike came along and took it. He has caught lots of big pike in this way.

It seems clear that far from insisting on a moving bait, pike are perfectly willing to pick a dead one off the bottom, and it seems to me that when the water is very cold, this might prove to be the very best way of fishing for them.

It used to be thought that the best weather for pike fishing was when it was very cold and frosty, but I never found it was so myself, and especially not for spinning. In such conditions, I should now try legering with a dead bait with a good deal of hope.

Arctic fish

An exception to much of what I have said about fishing in cold conditions is the grayling. I'd better mention that, in case I should mislead anyone. The grayling, of course, is really an arctic fish, left over from the Ice Age, and it revels in water so cold that only the current stops it from freezing.

17　I always carry a thermometer

Lots of chaps seem to think I'm joking when I tell them that I always have a thermometer with me when I go fishing. Others say that I'm being 'too scientific'; yet more, that it isn't any use because whatever the temperature I find, I can't change it.

In spite of all that I still carry my thermometer, because I know how much it has helped me to catch fish in the past, and I expect it to help me catch more in the future. If other chaps prefer old sayings like 'When the wind is in the east, then the fishes bite the least', and so on, they're welcome to them. I like something a bit more exact.

There are lots of theories and sayings about the effect of weather on fish; but having studied these effects for a good many years, and having also taken notice of the observations of many painstaking anglers, I've come to the conclusion (and it is after all, a very obvious conclusion) that the weather only affects the fish by affecting the water.

And that means that, except in so far as it may affect the water, the direction from which the wind is blowing makes no difference whatever to the fish. An east wind, for example, the one which is generally supposed to be the worst of the lot, might under certain circumstances prove a godsend if it sprang up at the right time.

That is where my thermometer can help—if it tells me that the water is too warm for fish to feed. I know that a wind, preferably a cool one, is going to help, and that I had better fish where it affects the water most if it comes. If, on the other hand, the water is a bit chilly, and the wind is chilly, too, I try to find a spot where the chilling effect of the wind is least, but if it happens to be a very warm wind which will raise the water temperature, I fish where it has the greatest effect.

Water temperature not only affects directly the activity of the fish, but also the amount of oxygen dissolved in the water, which the fish breathe. If my thermometer tells me that the water is so warm that there will be too little oxygen to suit some kinds of fish, I know I must look for places where there will be most oxygen, perhaps where there is disturbance by wind, or perhaps where a waterfall, weir, or spring increase oxygenation; perhaps where a bed of green weeds is giving off oxygen bubbles, if I want to catch fish of those kinds.

Having a thermometer doesn't mean ceasing to take notice of the weather; it means taking even more notice of it, for if you know the temperature of the water, you know how the weather is likely to affect it.

Sometimes, when you can predict what weather changes are due, you can both see and seize good chances to catch fish. But don't take any notice of the barometer, except as a means of helping to judge what weather to expect. I don't believe that atmospheric pressure affects fish directly—if they go a few feet deeper, the water pressure will change far more than the whole range of the household barometer. Fish have a mechanism to cope with far greater changes of pressure than that.

Let me give you an example of how a thermometer has actually helped me to catch good fish.

When I dealt with baits for carp some time ago in this column, I mentioned a couple of fish I had caught at Dagenham in 1952, in connection with the problem of overcoming a silk-weed-covered bottom, I didn't want to confuse the issue then, but actually there was more to catching those fish than the matters of choice of bait and making a long cast.

Before I began fishing that day, I walked all the way round the lake, taking the temperature at intervals, and in most places I found it was between 71 and 73°F.

Light breeze helped

Now, a considerable amount of observation by members of the Carp-catchers' Club and others has made us think that carp are disinclined to feed at temperatures over 68°F or so, probably because they begin to notice a shortage of oxygen then. That day was a sunny one, and there didn't seem much prospect of the water cooling to below 68°F before late evening or even the small hours of the following day.

But at about 10.30 am, a light breeze sprang up, blowing up the lake towards the shallow bay at the opposite end to the club hut, and by about 11.30 the temperature at that end, where there was a decided chop on the water, had fallen to 69°F. I cast out into the middle of that bay, and at 1.5 pm I got my first run, which resulted in the capture of a 22¾lb fish. The water temperature at 1.30 was 68°F, by 4.30 pm it had fallen to 67°F, and at that time I got another run from a 17½-pounder.

Although Harry Grief, Maurice Ingham, and I fished all through the following night and into the middle of the next morning, none of us had another bite, and, but for the information given by my thermometer, we wouldn't have had a fish at all.

That is only one among hundreds of cases where a thermometer has helped me to catch fish. It can help every angler in the same way. But any angler who wants it to help him must learn to apply the information it gives him. Temperature and oxygen affect different kinds of fish in different ways, and sometimes fish of the same species react somewhat differently in different waters, though the temperature may be the same.

To profit by the use of a thermometer therefore, an angler must keep using it all the time, until he has built up his own theories and ideas about what it can teach him.

I don't often offer advice to match anglers but I'll leave just one hint for their consideration.

Tip for matchmen

Often, in a match on a water where there are bream and roach, I have been faced with the choice of which to go for. If the bream are well on and there are some in my swim, I know that I stand a much better chance of winning if I set out to catch them. But how much time dare I spend in finding out if they will feed?

Very well. Directly the whistle blows, in goes my thermometer. In the waters I fish, I know pretty well what is the range of temperatures in which bream, if present in my swim, will feed keenly enough to be worth going after. If I find the temperature is under the lower limit, I forget about bream and go straight after roach, which will feed at much lower temperatures than bream.

And if the temperature is above the upper limit, I know that I am going to have a job to catch either roach or bream, and that I shall have to scratch for anything I can get, usually on ultra-fine tackle, maybe catching even bleak, gudgeon, or small perch and being glad to get them—unless, of course, chub are about.

Now, I'm not going to tell you what my upper and lower

limits of temperature are. They might be different on your waters, and you might disagree with my figures if you fished in mine. Perhaps, though you will agree that if you are keen to win matches it will pay you to get busy with a thermometer and decide on figures of your own.

18 Avoid cold spots

I have explained elsewhere some of the problems involved in fishing very shallow lakes. Very deep ones are easier in some ways, more difficult in others. To get the best results from deep lakes, you have to understand the relationship between depth, temperature, and wind.

Water is at its heaviest at a temperature of 39.2°F. So whenever the surface is at a lower temperature than that, the deepest place in the lake is also the warmest. On the other hand, once the temperature rises above 39.2°F, the deepest place is also the coldest. In winter, therefore, a thermometer tells you where to fish, because temperatures then are mostly fairly low and the fish seek the warmest places.

In summer, the water at the surface is often too warm for them, so they go deeper. But the temperature does not fall evenly with the depth. It does so up to a certain depth, then it falls very quickly through a small depth change of a few feet. This layer of water in which the sharp change of temperature takes place is called the thermocline.

Distance

Its distance from the surface varies with the time of year and the nature of the water. In a really big, deep lake it can go down to 40ft. But on some waters, it may not go below 15ft. Below it, the water is not only pretty chilly, but it may also be deoxygenated if there is a lot of decaying matter on the bottom. Water above the thermocline is reoxygenated by wind acting on the surface, but the water below the thermocline isn't. So you will not find fish there.

Wind has another effect. It tilts the thermocline, so that it is much deeper near the bank towards which the wind is blowing, and shallower at the side of the lake from the wind blows.

This means that in summer, you'll usually do better to fish with the wind in your face. Failure to understand this is one of the most common reasons for lack of success when fishing deep lakes. In a steady breeze that has been blowing for some hours, the thermocline may come right to the surface on the side of the lake from which the wind is blowing. You don't even need a thermometer to discover it. Put your hand in the water—it will feel icy. But remember, if the wind drops, which it usually does in the evening, the thermocline will tilt; it may even over-tilt. Then you can go back to the shore from which the wind blew earlier, and do well.

Another reason for fishing into the wind is that various insects get carried by the wind, beaten under by waves on the lee shore, and carried back and down by the undertow. This naturally attracts fish. I know that fishing in to the wind makes casting difficult, and waves interfere with bite detection, but if you want good catches, you have to put up with these difficulties. You won't catch fish where there aren't any. If you are fishing where there are plenty, you can afford to miss a lot of bites and still make a good catch.

And although casting into the wind is more difficult, you don't need to cast far, because the fish usually come quite close to the bank. They can't see you so easily in a wave. Once you've got your tackle out, you won't find the wind blows it back in as you might think. The undertow takes care of that for you.

Increases

Where the depth increases very quickly from the bank—that is, where the bottom slopes very steeply—you have to be careful how deep you fish, especially in calm conditions. I know a lake where it is more than 20ft deep 10yd out. In calm weather, if you fish on the bottom in 20ft you'll catch nothing. You have to fish between 8 and 12ft, in summer. That means either seeking a place where the bank shelves more gradually, or else fishing almost under the rod point. Fish will come in as close as that, if

66

neither you nor anyone else scares them. As this is a heavily fished water, there are usually careless people tramping around. So either you have to fish at odd times when fewest people are about, or else find one of the few places where the bottom slope is more gradual, so that you can fish farther out.

That shows how important it is to get to know a lake really well. It may take a whole day, or more, to plumb depths all round, but it pays off eventually.

Very deep

In very hot weather fish may be driven very deep indeed. In such conditions I've caught trout and perch in depths of 40ft. These fish had gone down as deep as the thermocline permitted, because that was the coolest place. There isn't much food at such depths, so when fish are driven there, they bite eagerly if you can get your bait to them. Again you see the importance of knowing your lake; in normal summer weather you may want to fish 8 to 12ft deep, but in a heatwave that has gone on for a week or more, you'll want to fish in much greater depths.

In the USA, where much more fishing on lakes is done from boats, anglers use electronic thermometers. They know which temperatures suit various species of fish best, and their thermometers tell them at what depth, on any day, these temperatures are to be found. In Britain, anglers are not willing to incur the expense of such devices, or adopt the attitude towards them that the Americans do.

But we can do reasonably well on big deep lakes if we remember the basic principles.

19 Finding the fish

A reader writes as follows: '. . . As a relative novice could I ask Mr Walker if he could tell me how I can find where, in a particular stretch of river, the fish are before starting to fish? . . .'

Well, I don't pretend that finding the fish is easy. In some waters, it's very difficult, which is all the more reason for taking time and trouble over it. Easy or difficult, it has to be done, because you can't catch fish unless you're fishing where they are.

How many rabbits would you succeed in shooting if you walked into a field blindfolded and let off a twelve-bore? Yet thousands of anglers expect to catch fish by casting into the first piece of open water they find.

Let's try to break down this business of fish finding into a logical sequence. There are several ways of finding fish. Here they are.

It's an art

1 By actually seeing the fish. If the water is sufficiently clear and shallow, you can see fish. Polarizing glasses help. There's an art in spotting fish, though.

Take your time. Look at a section or bottom and keep looking at it. At first you may see nothing, but as you watch you will probably see first one fish, then another. What at first looked like an orange coloured stone may be the anal fin of a big barbel. That bit of navy-blue rag—why, it's a chub's tail! Search the bottom, bit by bit. Place yourself to best advantage for the light and shade. Don't spend just a few minutes at it—spend hours. It's a good idea to give a day or two to this business in the close season when you can't fish anyway.

Many anglers tell me I have wonderful eyesight, because I've often seen fish that they had missed. My eyesight is no better than theirs; it's just a matter of knowing how to look and what to look for.

2 By watching for signs of fish. Under this heading I include fish that jump or roll at the surface, because although you do actually see the fish, it isn't done by looking into the water. There are other signs too, like showers of small fry jumping, bubbles coming to the surface, and stirred-up mud.

Watching for these signs takes time, but it is time well spent. Barbel leap in some waters, so do carp. Bream, roach, and tench roll on the surface, especially in the early morning and late evening.

Stir up mud

All bottom-feeding fish stir up mud at times, and carp, tench, and bream send up characteristic bubbles when feeding at the bottom. You can read about these habits in various books.

3 By carefully surveying the water and deducing which are the likeliest places for fish to occupy. You need to know depths, nature of bottom, position of weeds, set of current, overhead cover, and other things. Finding out about them takes time. Chub, roach, dace, and barbel like a hard bottom. Bream, carp, and tench like mud. There are exceptions, of course, which is something to remember because in angling there are very few hard-and-fast rules.

Deciding where fish will be, from what you know about what we might call the geography of the water, isn't infallible. Nobody is right every time, but the more information you can get, and the more you think about it, the more often will your bait be in the right place. What's more, this is an art in which you improve with practice.

In my opinion, there's nothing to beat making a rough sketch of a piece of water and noting down all you can discover on this sketch. Last time I suggested this, readers were scornful. To any who still are, I say OK, go ahead and fish at random, and then see how well you do. Me, I do all right, but I go to a lot of trouble. I don't expect to catch big fish without doing that.

More oxygen

4 By noting conditions of weather and water. The position fish occupy is often affected by such things as temperature, oxygen, and colour of water. If it is cold they move into deeper, slacker water in rivers, and deep holes in lakes and ponds. If it is hot, they move to where it is coolest or where there is most oxygen— often the same thing.

69

A weir or waterfall, or broken water, puts in more oxygen and fish may gather just below such places. In lakes, fish into the wind, in hot weather, casting where there's most 'chop'.

When water is much coloured, fish often feel safer and move into shallower swims where they'd be afraid to go if the water were clear.

5 *By considering food supplies and other attractions.* A simple case is where peas got into the river from a canning factory! Small, untreated sewage outfalls often attract fish. For example you'll catch plenty of chub if you trot down below the sewage outfall at Ross-on-Wye. And the sewage from Athlone attracts big bream shoals in the Shannon. I could give hundreds of similar examples.

As well as these man-made attractors, there are natural ones. Caterpillars falling from trees, elderberries falling from bushes, insects blowing against a bank, all may attract fish. Weed-beds hold countless aquatic insects, molluscs, and crustacea, and fish often wait around for what may come out or be washed out by the current.

Keep listening

6 *By keeping your ears open.* You'll hear other anglers talking about what they've seen, how they've done. 'Tom got smashed-up four times in the swim below the third willow.' 'Dick saw tremendous fishes rolling at dusk just above the stile.' 'Harry was puzzled because the mud was being stirred up on the shallow at the cattlebridge.' I don't need to tell you how to use such information!

Well, there it is. What I've written only touches the fringe of the subject; it would take a thick book to tell you all I know about finding fish. But what I want to stress is that you try hard to find the fish by all the ways you can think of, because it is by far the most important thing in fishing. Nothing else matters until you've done all you can to find where the fish are.

20 Groundbait correctly

We're always told that the faster the current, the farther upsteam we must throw our groundbait to ensure that it reaches bottom where we want it. That is not only an over-simplification of the problem, but it can actually be misleading.

I can remember, a very long time ago, timing how long maggots took to sink to the bottom of a bucket. From the figures I obtained, I worked out a table which was supposed to tell me just how far upsteam, from the place where I wanted the maggots to reach bottom, I ought to throw them in, for any combination of current speed and depth.

The whole thing was a complete waste of time, because I soon found out that above a certain speed of current, the maggots would never get to the bottom at all. As long as the current speed remained constant above that speed, the maggots would continue to be carried on downstream. That applies not only to maggots, but to any other kind of groundbait. Of course, the speed of current above which the groundbait keeps on going down is different for different kinds of groundbait.

Something heavy, like wheat, will get down where maggots or bread pulp would be carried on by the stream for miles. But if the current is fast enough, even wheat will be carried on and fail to reach bottom, no matter how far upstream you put it in. Another factor that has to be taken into consideration, with such groundbaits as damp sausage rusk, powdered bread, bread and bran, or bread and barley meal, is the size of the lump you throw in.

The bigger the lump, the quicker it will reach bottom, if it is going to reach bottom at all. And where loose groundbait would go downstream without reaching bottom for miles, the same stuff squeezed into a big tight ball, will go down and stay down.

It pays to remember that, except in a turbulent stream, the surface current is always greatest, and if you can get your groundbait down through the surface rush, it will sink into slower water and stay where you want it. This is specially important where shallow runs deepen into pools. It's no good throwing loose light groundbait into the shallow fast water above the pool if you want it to settle at the upstream end of the deeper water. It will probably go right down the pool with the surface current, and if it settles at all, it will be at the tail of the pool, provided the water there doesn't speed up too much. What is wanted for such a place is a very heavy groundbait that will go nearly straight down through the surface current at the head of the pool.

It has been said that groundbait that is being carried downstream in a deep swim will settle at the tail, where the swim begins to get shallower, but actually it seldom does anything of the kind. At the tail, since the depth is less but the volume of water going down is the same, the current speeds, and away goes the groundbait at increased pace.

Now, if you stop and think about all that, you'll realize that except in a very slow river, it is very difficult indeed to get the right groundbait in the right place. The essential thing to realize about groundbait is that unless you know exactly where it is and can put your baited hook among it, or near it, you are actually handicapping yourself badly. You're attracting fish away from your bait. Haphazard groundbaiting is far, far worse than no groundbaiting at all.

That explains the relative success of the swim-feeder. Although the tiny quantity of maggots or groundbait that a swim-feeder can hold is nowhere near enough to really attract and hold a big shoal of fish, that small amount is at least put exactly where it will be most effective. Without some such device, nine anglers out of ten wouldn't be fishing within several yards of where their groundbait reached bottom, if it ever reached bottom at all.

In any current above a crawl, therefore, if you want groundbait on the bottom, put it in big, tight lumps. If you want light stuff like maggots or cloud in it, make a cup of heavy material, like bread and barley meal, put the light stuff inside, along with a stone or two, and mould some more heavy stuff over the opening. Get it good and tight, and at least as big as a cricket ball. And where conditions permit, throw it in attached to your hook. Don't cast it with your rod; coil some line and lob out by hand.

When you tighten up, you'll know pretty well where that groundbait is. Pull your line free, bait your hook, and you can fish with some confidence. If you're afraid the ball won't break up quickly enough, you can put some dry sausage rusk inside, but remember to try to keep the whole thing really heavy. As the sausage rusk gets damp, it will swell up and burst the groundbait ball.

For very fast water, a solid ball of soaked stale bread with as much water squeezed out as possible before pounding and kneading, does very well, and takes quite a time to disintegrate in the current. You can prolong its effectiveness by working into it some boiled wheat, only boiled for about half the time you'd boil it for hook bait. Or if you're after chub, you can include some dried peas that have been well soaked and boiled until soft, but not nearly to the stage where they split. These will spread on the bottom after the bread part has been washed away.

Of course, you don't always want groundbait to reach bottom. There are times when a steady trickle of bread pulp or maggots down a swim will bring chub, dace, roach, and other fish a long way upstream, and a float tackle trotted down in the line taken by the groundbait will account for plenty of fish. In that kind of fishing, the quantity used is all-important, and only local knowledge allied with commonsense will tell you the correct rate at which to put the groundbait in. Too high a rate for the number of fish will take them downstream, perhaps beyond your reach. Too low a rate will not attract enough. Usually, it pays to err on the moderate side.

I could write a whole book about groundbaiting, and still not cover the subject properly, but I do want to stress how very important it is to do your groundbaiting, and baiting-up correctly.

If you can't, you'd better not groundbait at all.

Part Three:
The Fish

21 How to stalk the timid chub

If you want to catch a big chub, you need to know as much as possible about how they behave. A chub is a lazy fish, and although he can swim with ease against very fast currents, he doesn't do it if he needn't. So you'll usually find him out of the main current, in slower water or even in a dead slack.

He is also a very timid fish, the easiest of all fish to scare. And even if he isn't scared, he doesn't like to be far away from cover, such as willow roots, branches that have fallen into the water, rush-beds, lily-pads, anything that offers safe shelter. He would rather be over a gravel or sand bottom, but he'll settle for clay or even mud if everything else is satisfactory.

He can see you at a greater distance than any other fish, and he can also detect a knock on the bank, or on the bottom of a boat, better. The commonest reason for failure to catch big chub is that the angler is scaring them. Always provided, that is, that he has found where the big chub are, which few anglers ever do, because the bigger chub are seldom found in the deep weed-free stretches of rivers that most anglers choose to fish.

The chub is also a fish that doesn't need telling twice what he had better avoid. Consequently, although an uneducated chub will eat almost anything, a chub seldom reaches a weight of 5 or 6lb without learning that there are kinds of food best left alone.

Here is a list of baits on which I have caught chub. Cheese paste, cheese cubes, bread paste, bread crust, bread flake, corn-flakes, beans, luncheon meat, sausage, congealed blood, raw liver, pork fat, suet, lobworms, brandlings, black slugs, white slugs, crayfish, small whole fish, pieces of fish, caddis grubs, dock grubs, caterpillars, maggots, houseflies, blowflies, daddy-long-legs, beetles, bumble bees, cherries, snowberries, tomato, banana, macaroni, hempseed, stewed wheat, plugs, artificial flies, spoons, devon minnows, silkweed, lamprey larvae, dead frogs, mayfly nymphs, peas, egg yolk paste, mussel, grasshoppers, and grapes. I expect there are more that I've forgotten. So wherever you find a big chub that refuses the bait you are offering him, because he knows it isn't safe, you will have plenty of alternatives to try.

Very few chub are scared of tackle. They're just as willing to take a bait on a No 6 hook, tied to a 6, 7, or even 8lb line, as on a smaller hook and a finer line. Which is just as well, because most big chub live in spots where you need stout tackle to get 'em out.

So when you read the match reports, which tell how someone caught half a dozen chub up to $3\frac{1}{2}$lb on a $1\frac{1}{2}$lb line and a size 20 hook, and must have won if he hadn't been broken once or twice, don't be encouraged to use similar tackle. How often do you read of a chub over 5lb being landed in a match? We're talking about catching big chub, remember! If I had to be limited to one hook size and one line strength for chub, I'd choose a No 6 on a 6lb line, and then I'd expect to be smashed-up occasionally.

But chub can sometimes be very cunning, for although they don't seem to care whether a bait is on fine or stout nylon, some of the craftier ones know whether a bait is attached to a line or not. Carp that have learned this leave the bait alone, but chub sneak up, take the bait, cut the line and depart, without the line moving. You wind in and find the hook is missing. If this happens, wait half an hour, then cast into the same spot and when the bait has sunk, draw it back as slowly as possible. If you feel a check, strike.

Slow retrieve

Another odd thing about chub is that unlike any other members of the carp family they'll often take a bait which is being reeled upstream. So if you're free-lining or long-trotting, bring your tackle back slowly through the swim.

Earlier in this article I explained that chub like places where there is cover nearby and where the current is such that they can take life easily. If you want to catch big ones you must seek these spots, and the most successful catchers of big chub are those anglers who spend more time looking for the right places than actually fishing.

It doesn't take long to catch a chub. From the time you cast until the fish is on the bank is often no more than ten minutes. So it is well worth spending plenty of time walking quietly and stealthily along the river bank, looking out for places where big chub might be.

On a bright day you can sometimes see the fish just under the surface, even in rivers that are coloured.

There's hardly any time of day or night when chub won't bite, and they'll feed when the water is too warm or too cold for most other species. But like many other kinds of fish, they usually bite best at dusk, and again at dawn, though the biggest handicap you have to contend with is the behaviour of other anglers, who scare the fish before you can catch them. So it pays, whenever possible, to fish when and where the fewest number of other people are about. I can truthfully say that my score of big chub would be double what it is, but for the fish-scaring activities of other people.

Quite often you find a big chub or two in a spot that is impossible to reach, because of branches, rushes, or reeds. Take a look around, to see if there is a more accessible spot into which those fish will move, either of their own accord or through the temptation of a bit of groundbait, after the sun is off the water.

Chub often move into very shallow water from their daytime lies, once the sun has fallen below that magic angle of $10°$. I've taken them from water hardly deep enough to cover their backs. In very hot weather, that has stayed that way for several days, chub will move into broken water, either below weirs and waterfalls, or where there are rocks and boulders to break up the flow. You can't usually pick out extra large specimens in such conditions, but if you fish these areas you often get a big fish among the smaller ones.

You fish free-line, and bait with a bit of tough crust from the bottom of a tin loaf. It gets drawn down and whirled about in the turbulent water. To look at these places you'd think no fish could live in them, let alone see and take a bait. But they do.

Best of all, though, is spotting a big chub in a place where you can creep up unobserved and flick a bait to him, watching him loom up, open his big white mouth, and chomp it as it strikes. I find this one of the most exciting things in all angling, and even after all the years I've spent after chub, I still find it difficult to restrain myself from striking too soon or too violently. Wait till your fish has shut his mouth and turned away, then tighten firmly and keep a good pressure on.

It's nice to know that there are only a few rivers in England, southern Scotland, and parts of Wales that don't hold big chub.

22 Chub and the crust

I suppose most anglers with chub fishing experience know the value of what has been described as 'free-line' fishing.

This is casting a good-sized bait on a line that has neither float nor weight of any sort except that of the baited hook itself. This is a very deadly way to catch chub in summer, especially where you can actually see the fish. You spot a chub, or a group of chub, and you cast the bait so that it drops where they can see it. Unless it's a bait on which one or more of them have been caught before, and unless they've been scared by seeing you or the flash of your rod, or by your footfalls, it's odds on you get a bite. You can also search likely spots with this method casting out and watching for any movement of the line that would indicate a bite.

There are some variations on this method, though, that aren't quite so well known. One is using a floating crust. At one time this had quite a vogue on parts of the Hampshire Avon, but as the summer holiday crowds increased it failed, probably because no self-respecting chub dare show its nose in the circumstances. On waters where the banks are not so crowded floating crust can still catch summer chub, and big ones, too. What's more, it can help you find them. What you do is send down crust cubes, loose, till you see them being taken. Then down goes the one with a hook in it!

Unless they've been scared, chub will cheerfully come to the surface and take a floating crust, and there aren't many more exciting moments in fishing than when your crust, floating down the current perhaps 30 or 40yd away, suddenly disappears with a great suck and swirl and you hit something heavy with a solid thud. You need a fresh crust for every swim down, of course, but there are days when you can really hammer the chub.

Never be afraid of letting your crust run down rapids or broken water. It's hard to believe, when you see a fat old chub lazing about in a bit of slack, that the same fish can live happily in water so turbulent that when you're near it you'd have to raise your voice to make your mate hear. Well, he can. I've had 5lb chub out of rapids that made a permanent rainbow. They

Small baits, fished hard on the bottom, are usually the most effective way of catching fish when the river bank is fringed with snow and ice

(overleaf) Swims like this with a relatively heavy weed growth make ideal holding spots for big fish of all species. The weed provides both food and shelter for the fish and gives the angler a chance to land a specimen fish, provided he is prepared to use suitable tackle

Rod aloft, Dick Walker lands a fighting barbel from the Hampshire Avon

(opposite above) The author nets a good bream from a Lincolnshire lake; *(opposite below)* bending the rod into a big fish after the strike has been made can often secure a shaky hookhold. Modern nylon line and the flexibility of fibreglass rods reduce the danger of line breakage to a minimum

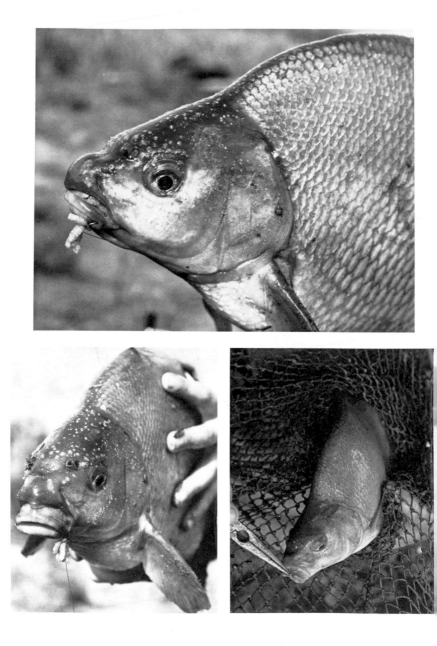

Big bream have mouths to match with tough, leathery lips. Hooks have to be driven home . . . and sometimes have to be removed with the aid of pliers or artery forceps

(above) A youthful author with a big chub, lured on crust, from the River Wye;
(below) a typical fen drain, straight and almost featureless. A careful approach
by the angler will often be rewarded by a catch of specimen fish

(*above*) A small pike is lifted ashore on a large Midlands reservoir. The species can reach giant proportions, with fighting qualities to match; (*below*) barbel like this can often be the reward for a November barbel outing. But choose a muggy, overcast day and not a bright, sunny one

(*above*) The fish for which Dick Walker is best known—his record carp. The 44lb fish, or 'Clarissa' as she was later christened, is held by Pete Thomas, Dick's fishing companion at the time of capture; (*below*) the end result of a properly planned carp session—a double-figure fish safely netted. It is vital to choose the right time and place to fish and to keep bankside disturbance to a minimum

(above) A specimen perch taken on a spinner. Big worms and small fish also make fine baits; *(below)* a fine brace of summer tench taken by the lift method

(opposite) A beaten grayling is brought to the net. This fish, from the River Ure in Yorkshire, fell to float-fished maggot

The author makes a long cast at a Hampshire trout fishery. Choosing the correct rod for your style of trout fishing is an essential ingredient of success; *(above right)* Dick Walker with a superbly marked rainbow trout of 18lb 14oz. The fish was

taken from Avington fishery, Hampshire and fell to a Partridge and Orange fly, fished on a 6lb point

Bait: *(above left)* maggots, although a fine all-round bait for most species of fish, have one major disadvantage for the specimen hunter—they are too easily taken by unwanted small fish; *(above right)* hempseed, a deadly bait for many species of fish. The seed is harmful to neither fish nor waters; *(below left and right)* bread flake is an attractive, all-season bait for most species of coarse fish. Samples like this are ideal for big chub, barbel, bream and tench

(above left) Wheat is a deadly autumn bait for roach, dace and bream; *(above right)* worms are a deadly and inexpensive bait which will lure almost every species of coarse fish. The different types and sizes, ranging from the large lobworm to the small cockspur, provide the angler with a size of bait for every kind of fishing condition; *(below)* good groundbaiting can be the key to catching fish consistently. Carefully prepared groundbait like this can actually prevent the angler from catching fish if it doesn't end up in the right part of the swim

(*above*) This 11lb 2oz eel is conclusive proof that double-figure specimens can be landed on rod and line. Captor Steve Perry holds the fish which has been accepted as a British record; (*below*) the habits and formations of roach shoals can vary enormously from one water to another. Sometimes the fish in the shoal are all the same size, on other waters the shoal may contain fish of mixed sizes

lie in the shelter of the big stones and boulders and they can be out and back with your crust like lightning.

There are sweltering summer days when you can catch chub in broken water and nowhere else. The bites are hard to detect; half the time you can't see your crust, and the current makes all sorts of tugs and jerks on your line. You will have bites you know nothing about, you'll strike at what you think are bites, but aren't, and you'll miss bites that are good solid ones. But you'll catch chub, and in water of that sort you'll be amazed at the scrap they put up. Even one of a pound feels like a monster. After a while you develop a sort of instinct and this tells you when to strike.

Because of the turmoil, the chub can't see you very easily and it would take a very heavy tread to scare them. So don't assume you've finished after catching a fish or two, as you would have in most summer chub swims. You can easily catch twenty chub from a stretch of rapids—if they're there.

The floating crust is far and away the most effective way of fishing rapids and broken water; in fact, it might not be exaggerating too much to say that there are places where it's the only way you could fish.

Another variation of the free-line method is the bait that is cast downstream, beyond where the chub are or are thought to be, and then pulled upstream. It sounds logical enough when the bait is a crayfish hooked by the tail or a minnow, gudgeon, or roach. All these could swim up the current by themselves in a natural state. Of course chub will take them so, and it's a very killing method of fishing.

There are two curious things about it, though. There are times when chub won't look at a bait coming up the current, but will have it like a shot when it's allowed to drift down, And there are other days when they just ignore a bait drifting down, but hit it savagely when it is drawn up. Don't ask me why, but it does happen so, and the wise chub fisher knows it and if one way doesn't work he tries the other.

The other queer thing is that when chub are hitting the bait as it is reeled up against the current, they'll hit cheese paste or lobworms. Neither of these do much natural swimming upstream! It's difficult to think of anything as unnatural as a piece of cheese paste swimming up the river; but the chub don't worry. I've taken far more chub when fishing for them on the

Wye with cheese or worms wound upstream than I ever have by any other method.

There's no bite detection problem here! And it is no method for find tackle, either, a 4lb chub hits with a force that can take the rod clean out of your hand. The line is tight from rod to bait, of course, so hold the rod horizontal but pointing slightly upsteam so that its bend can take the stock. You'll be smashed-up more often than you'll like it, if you don't.

If you're going to pull cheese paste upstream mould it into a bomb shape to slip easily through the water. It won't wash off as easily then. Let the hook-point stand well out, or you'll miss a lot of bites.

Some people advocate trebles for the job and I think it would probably help, but I don't care to use trebles for anything but pike or salmon myself. If you're running a lobworm upstream, and you are missing good pulls, try a two-hook tackle with a No 12 at the head of the worm and a No 6 at the tail. And if it's a salmon river you're fishing, well you may get what feels like a very exceptional chub indeed—but isn't!

23 Striking for tough-mouthed bream

David Ashby's letter to the *Angling Times*, in which he asked for advice about catching big bream in gravel pits, is only one of many that have come in from readers who have similar problems, so I'm going to try here to sort some of them out. Boiled down to essentials, what these readers are saying is 'We don't hook 'em often enough, and when we do they nearly always get rid of the hook somehow!'

So there are really two problems, the first of which is how to get more bites.

In waters that are fairly extensive, bream usually keep well away from the banks, especially where there are large numbers of anglers. So it pays to develop techniques suitable for fishing at ranges of from 25yd or so upwards.

You can't do this successfully with float tackle carrying one or two BB shot. Either you must use leger tackle, or else a fairly large float that will carry two or three swan-shot. Because of the effects of wind and drift on the line, it is best to use a float attached by the bottom end only, and to sink most of the line between it and the rod, if you really think a float is necessary. In deep water, of course, a slider would be needed. But stillwater bream usually give quite definite bites on leger tackle. If the bottom is clear, a simple leger will serve; if there is a lot of silkweed, the lead will have to be on a link at least as long as the depth of the silkweed.

The main advantage of the float is that it shows you exactly where your tackle is, and therefore makes accurate groundbaiting easier. If you leger, you need a landmark on the opposite bank, and a marker on your line, to be sure that your hookbait and groundbait are in the same place. Even when using float tackle, it is advantageous to put the lead on a link where there is much silkweed; but of course it is better to tackle the silkweed problem by removing it if possible, and groundbaiting the cleared spot.

Regular groundbaiting, or baiting-up if you'd rather call it that, helps enormously in catching bream, specially when you can't be sure that your chosen pitch is on the route taken by some of the bream shoals. If you can go to that water and bait-up every day for a week, your chances are improved enormously.

Feeding times of bream are unpredictable and fish are sometimes taken at midday, but the likeliest times on most waters are dusk, dawn, and through the night. A would-be bream catcher must experiment with fishing times until he can detect some kind of feeding pattern on the water he fishes. Never assume that failure to get bites means the bream aren't in your swim. I've seen sixty or seventy big bream swimming round and around my bait for hours but ignoring it. Then suddenly they decide to take it, and I've had fish after fish for the next hour or so. They will stop feeding as suddenly as they started, too.

It is also worth experimenting with baits and groundbaits. On some waters, you can catch big bream on bread paste; on others, big worms are much more successful. On one lake I used to fish, any kind of bread bait was entirely useless; all the bream wanted was big worms.

On another, I caught plenty of big bream on paste, while all I got on lobs was small perch and eels. Sometimes bream will bite readily on small worms like cock-spurs or brandlings, or on lively marshworms, when lobworms or paste are ignored. And sometimes the bream will bite on any bait you care to put on the hook.

The curious thing is that even where bread hook baits fail, bread or meal groundbaits still attract the fish, though for baiting-up in advance, it's a good idea to put worms in the groundbait, or throw in balls of earth with plenty of worms held inside them.

So much for getting bites; now for the problem of fish that get rid of the hook. This is something that I've encountered with fish of all kinds, from enormous carp down to moderate-sized roach. I have now come to the firm opinion that except when using very tiny hooks that can tear out, the reason why fish shed hooks is that the hooks were never driven fully home in the first place.

Far from having tender mouths, bream, especially big ones, have very tough mouths indeed. Hammer a No 6 into the mouth of a 9lb bream, and you'll need pliers or surgical forceps to get it out. The last time I was catching bream of that size or bigger, I broke four or five hooks while trying to extract them.

Few anglers realize how feeble is the effect of a strike. I advise everyone to test this for himself. Get a friend to stand 20 or 30yd away, holding your rod while you hold the end of the line. Ask him to strike. You'll be amazed at the feebleness of the pull you feel.

A combination of a fibreglass rod, stretchy nylon, and a not-too-sharp hook can make effective hooking at such ranges almost impossible. So for this kind of fishing, use a split cane* rod, make sure your hook is dead sharp, and hammer bites hard. Really hard. And use a line that lets you do it without risk of breakage. I usually use 5lb or 6lb line for this sort of work, not because it's needed to avoid breakage while playing a bream, but to allow a really powerful strike.

For some kinds of fish, and especially in weedy or snaggy

* Modern fibreglass rods are satisfactory

waters where those fish have to be stopped, you need a very strong hook, but this isn't necessary for stillwater bream, which are not strong fighters. For them, I use a fine wire hook of the kind called Bussy d'Amboise, made by Mustads. This type of hook, which is spade-ended, has excellent penetrating qualities, particularly after being touched-up with a fine sharpening stone. Nos 4 or 6 will do for lobworms or paste, and No 8 for brandlings.

A 10ft split-cane rod, like the Mk IV Avon, ought to be quite satisfactory for stillwater work where the line is reasonably straight between rod and bait, but a rod 2ft longer, which is much better for long range river fishing where the current puts a big bow in the line, is no handicap when fishing lakes and gravel pits, provided it has plenty of backbone.

It doesn't matter if it is a bit heavy, you aren't going to sit holding it anyway. What does matter is that it must have the power to pick up a lot of sunken, stretched nylon and hammer a hook in right over the barb.

24 How to catch big bream

I believe 1974 promises to be an exceptionally good season for big bream. So here are some of the things to remember if you're keen to catch a bream of specimen size.

First, there is no best time to fish.

Most anglers believe that late evening, through the night, and early morning are the best times to fish for bream, and I think that to a certain extent they're right. But some of the biggest catches my friends and I have made, both in terms of numbers and size of individual fish, have come in the middle of the day. What's more, we've caught them in bright hot weather. So although it is wise to plan your fishing to allow late evening and early morning sessions, don't forget that there's always a chance at any time of day or night.

I hesitate to try to guess how many hours I've put in after big bream, but the experience gained from them leads me to think that the worst time of all is between about 11 pm and 3 am in summer. So if night fishing is not allowed on your waters, don't worry. If they'll only let you fish up to an hour before sunset, you won't miss much sport.

Next, it's a fact that bream can eat a lot of groundbait and in most waters using a lot, correctly, helps to increase your catch more than with any other species of fish. There are several common mistakes made by anglers who groundbait for bream. First, because a lot is needed, people tend to choose rubbishy material. Far better, if you're worried about cost, to use less good stuff than a lot of bad stuff.

Not mouldy

Stale bread is good, so long as it isn't mouldy. Soak it really thoroughly, and then mash it up equally thoroughly, or you'll find half of it floats and drifts away. Pour off the surplus water, then add enough proprietary cereal groundbait to dry it off to the stage where balls the size of an orange will hold together till they hit the water, for lake work. For rivers, you need a tighter binder, such as barley meal or wholemeal flour (not the self-raising sort).

Take all the time, trouble and experimenting you need to get it right for the water you're fishing because bad groundbaiting is far worse than no groundbaiting at all.

The alternative to cereal groundbait is worms, either big ones or small ones, but don't use both at the same time. For river fishing, put the worms into clay balls; for lakes, put them in soft mud. Whether you use worms or cereal depends on the water. If it teems with small rudd and roach, but holds few or no eels, use worms. But if eels and small perch are numerous, you'll be better off with cereal.

I don't rate maggots as highly as most bream anglers. But if you do decide to use them, it'll cost you, because a few pints are useless. You want several gallons to do the job properly.

The next common fault in groundbaiting is failure to make sure you can put your baited hook among the groundbait, every time. It stands to reason that if you can't, all your groundbait will do is attract fish away from your hook. In lake fishing, especially, it is all too easy to bait up at extreme range and then, when you come to fish, to find a headwind has sprung up and you can't cast as far as you need to, or else that when you arrive at dusk or early dawn, in poor light, you haven't a clue how far out the groundbait really is.

So before the groundbait goes in, fix up float tackle and cast it out at a distance you know you can repeat whatever the conditions. Then put a marker on your line, so you'll always know exactly how far out that was. Leave the tackle out, so that you can use the float as an aiming point when you throw out the groundbait.

In actual fishing, you may have to leger, but the line marker will still give your distance. You can make allowance for the extra line involved in float-fishing as compared to legering, and in any case your groundbaiting won't be all that accurate. In fact it pays to spread it around somewhat, to allow for errors in casting.

Tackle

Bream aren't great fighters, but they do offer a lot of resistance to the strike, so don't fish too fine. In completely open water, 4lb to 5lb is about right. If you have to work your fish through weed or lily pads, make it 6lb. A No 6 hook does for big lobworms; No 8 for breadflake, and No 10 for a bunch of small red worms or brandlings. Don't take any notice of what the match fishers tell you about the need for fine tackle. I've caught dozens of big bream accidentally on 12lb lines and No 2 hooks while carp fishing. When they're really on the feed, they won't be put off by 6lb line and No 6 hooks.

Which spots should you choose to bait and to fish? Answer—if possible where you see bream rolling on the surface, or where you see the water is carrying more colour than elsewhere. Time spent looking for such places is never wasted, but if you can't see either indication don't despair because bream shoals wander about a lot and if you groundbait properly, you have a good chance of attracting them to where you want them, specially if you can bait up for several days in a row.

I like to use an antenna float of good size for lake fishing, when there's light enough to see it; otherwise I leger, and I've got no time for fancy bite indicators then. Nothing beats a Beta-light bobbin, clipped on the line between butt ring and reel, or on the line between two rod-rings, for bream fishing in the dark though confirmed addicts may like to tape a Beta-light bobbin on the swing tip.

Remember, bream will start feeding all of a sudden, and then stop equally suddenly. And it isn't simply a case of the shoal arriving and then departing. Your bait can lie plumb in the middle of a shoal for hours, without being taken; then suddenly the bream will decide to feed and you'll get bite after bite.

On the drop

If you keep missing bites, you're probably not getting proper bites, but bream are running into your line. If that happens, try increasing the distance between float and lead, and after casting, wind the bait back a bit; try to fish it on the nearer side of the shoal. You want to avoid these 'line-bites' as far as possible because not only do they cause a lot of striking and missing, they can also scare the fish and even cause the shoal to depart.

With cereal groundbait and flake or paste hook-bait, it is possible for the groundbait to be so stirred up by fish moving about, that they start taking it from above the bottom. It you were fishing in daylight, with a float, you'd then expect bites 'on the drop' and fish accordingly. With the leger used after dark, you can't do that, so what you do instead is bait with crust, a fairsized piece, which will float up as far above the bottom and lead. Sometimes this distance can be as much as a foot; more often 3 or 4in.

This is definitely the way to fish over a bottom of very soft mud or silkweed, in any case.

Don't worry if you're pestered with small fish at first. They'll soon move out when the bream move in, and you'll start getting those lovely slow bites, I hope, that you could hardly miss if you tried.

25 Do barbel need fast water to thrive?

The capture of a 12lb barbel from the river Nene, a river not previously thought suitable for this species, makes me wonder if the generally accepted ideas about what sort of water barbel like are really correct.

I have spent hundreds of hours watching barbel of all sizes up to 20lb or so, in clear water. They can hold their position in very fast water indeed, of that there is no doubt. But do they really need fast water in order to thrive?

In recent years, many of the big barbel caught from the Hampshire Avon have come from the slacks. Still more have come from stretches of the Thames and from backwaters and tributaries of that river, where the current is either slow, very slow, or nil.

Where I have been able to watch barbel in the Hampshire Avon and in the Kennet, both relatively fast rivers, I have usually found that although the water at the surface of the swims in which they live is moving quickly, the barbel at the bottom have chosen resting places where they are protected from the push of water. They lie in slacks behind big stones, or at the tail-ends of big bunches of streamer weed, or where a sharp drop in the river bed causes a pocket of slow water to form.

What I think makes fast rivers specially suitable for barbel is that they probably need fast water over clean gravel in order to breed successfully. If you look, you can usually find such places here and there, even in rivers like the Nene and the Great Ouse that are, generally speaking, slow.

The Great Ouse, of course, holds quite a large number of barbel, far more than most anglers who fish it are willing to believe. What's more, they breed successfully. Long-standing readers may remember a centre-page feature I produced for *Angling Times*, about how Ian Howcroft and Chuck Nunn devoted many successive weekends in their attempt to locate and catch barbel from the Great Ouse. And they did finally succeed in catching several small ones, quite young fish that must have been bred in the river, not introduced from elsewhere.

Ian and Chuck also hooked larger fish which succeeded in breaking away, mainly due to the snaggy bottom of the deep weir pool in which they were hooked. I have caught barbel in the Ouse, including a 9lb fish, so it is clear that they can grow to good size there and there must be quite a lot of double-figure fish in it by now.

As in the Nene, most anglers who fish the river are unlikely to catch these fish. Few fish in the spots that barbel inhabit; few fish with the baits that barbel are likely to take; and even fewer use tackle that would give them much chance of landing a big barbel, even if they hooked one.

I know that in the past, big barbel have been successfully landed on fragile tackle, but there's a lot of difference in deliberately fishing for barbel with a size 14 hook and 3lb line, and hooking a big barbel that unexpectedly takes your bait on the same tackle, when you're fishing for roach or bream.

One other thing that affects the issue is that the fewer anglers there are fishing deliberately for barbel in a given stretch of water, the harder they are to catch. You have only to look at the situation in the Hampshire Avon to realize the truth of this.

On that river, barbel are by no means confined to the Royalty fishery. There are lots of barbel all the way up the river, to above Downton; yet very few barbel are caught except from

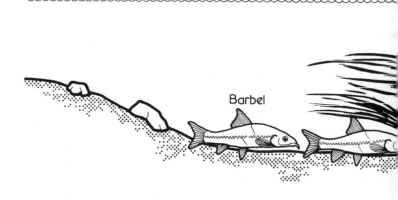

Barbel

the Royalty. You can find them fairly easily in other parts of the river, but it is next to impossible to persuade them to take a bait. The only difference between the Royalty and these other stretches of the Avon is the amount of free feed that goes in. Hundreds of gallons of maggots per week go into the Royalty. Nothing remotely comparable goes in anywhere else in the Avon.

Before maggot mania took over on the Royalty, stones and stones of cheese, bread, and bran were used instead. Whatever bait anglers throw into the Royalty is of sufficient quantity to be an important proportion of the feed available to the fish. Eating maggots is part of their way of life. Consequently they take maggots that are on anglers' hooks. In other parts of the river, they don't know what a maggot is!

I am convinced that to get barbel to take any bait freely, it is necessary for free samples of that bait to be put into the water in large quantities and at frequent intervals. This is not, of course, a new idea. When Victorian anglers wanted to catch barbel from the Thames, they employed professional fishermen to bait up suitable swims with something like five to ten thousand lobworms, spread over as long as a fortnight in advance of fishing day.

On some waters, the chances of catching barbel without any such extensive and expensive preparations are rather

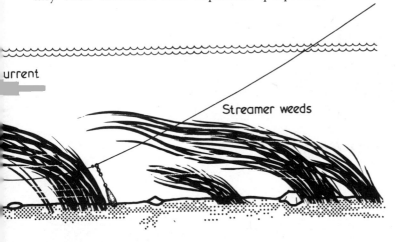

current

Streamer weeds

A typical barbel lie at the tail-end of bunches of streamer weed

better because the barbel are more accustomed to getting various foodstuffs without anglers having to provide them. In some rivers where there is a considerable variation in flow, lots of worms get washed in.

Not on the Hampshire Avon, be it noted! That is fed from the chalk springs and apart from the occasional winter floods, the variation in level is small. And on top of that, the soil of the banks holds few worms, as anyone who has scratched about to find one knows well enough.

In recent years, Thames anglers have been catching quite a few barbel on such baits as sausage and pieces of tinned meat. If you consider the number of craft on the Thames nowadays on which meals are prepared, and add the various riverside dwelling from which plate-scrapings and other food wastes may find their way into the river, you may not be surprised that barbel should have learned that sausage meat and spam make good eating.

Of this I am sure, if you want to catch barbel from rivers like the Nene and the Great Ouse, you will have to set about the job methodically, and not expect to catch them without a good deal of investigation and preparation, and probably, a large measure of disappointment.

I am equally sure that success is unlikely to come from the use of some exotic bait. It will be a case of finding where the barbel are and then educating them, over a period of many days, perhaps even weeks to take some simple, easily obtained bait like worms, maggots, cheese, or sausage.

26 Warm and muggy—then go for barbel

If you check through old copies of angling journals you'll find that early November has produced lots of really big barbel, and you may conclude that autumn is a good time to fish for them.

Well, it is and it isn't. The truth is that it all depends on the day. Autumn conditions are so very variable.

On the side of the angler is the fact that natural food in the river is scarcer. If the water is still at a reasonably high temperature, the barbel will be hungry, the natural food supply less, and the chances of a barbel taking your bait will be better, provided you can fish the bait correctly where the barbel will find it.

Unfortunately, that isn't always so easy. Very likely you'll be cursed with fallen leaves coming down the current, giving lots of 'false knocks' on your leger tackle and eventually clinging to your line in such numbers that the increased current drag, pulls your leger out of position. Worse still, you may find that a rise in the river is washing down bits of dead, broken-off rush and weed, which have the same effect as submerged dead leaves, only much more so.

Of course, although these troubles are bad enough, things can be worse. A severe overnight frost may knock the water temperature down several degrees and then the barbel won't feed at all. Nor will anything else, except grayling and perhaps an odd chub or dace. If you find the water has turned an odd sea-green colour, like the edge of a bit of plate glass, your chances of sport are extremely poor.

What leads to disappointment for those lucky anglers who can choose which days they like to fish, is a spell of what everyone calls fine autumn weather; bright sunny days warm enough to make you sweat if you have to carry your tackle far. The first day in a spell of this kind of weather is usually all right, but that's not the day anglers usually choose. No, they wait till the second or third fine day.

Now, although in these fine autumn spells the sun is lovely and warm from perhaps 10.30 am until 5 pm, the night following such a day is nearly always a very cold one indeed, with a lot of frost. So although the weather next day looks lovely, the chances of sport are poor in rivers and shallow lakes.

In such weather conditions, I'd prefer to forget about barbel and indeed river and shallow lake fishing altogether, and instead, go and see what a lob on a size 6 will do at the bottom of 30 or 40ft of water in a deep gravel pit or reservoir.

Coloured water

The best weather for autumn fishing, not only for barbel but other river species, and particularly for perch, is warm muggy weather, with the sky completely covered with cloud and as often as not, moisture falling of the sort that can't make up its mind whether it is rain or mist. If that kind of weather persists for two or three days, it's a very good time to go river fishing. There will have been enough moisture, as like as not, to increase the flow a bit without causing spate conditions. There'll be a bit of colour in the water, but not a lot of mud.

Of course, you may very well have to contend with leaves and bits of weed, but there are ways of minimizing their nuisance value. You can look for a swim downstream from a jutting piece of bank, where the leaves and rubbish are deflected out across the river and a clearer space is left under your own bank.

Remember, when there is a small rise in level and an increase in colour, barbel often move close in under the bank. And when they do, they are more willing than at any other time to take a worm, which is a very likely kind of natural food for them to expect in such circumstances. Note that after an overnight frost, the opposite is true. Worms will be deep in the soil and a lot of moisture will be locked into the ground, so the river won't have risen and coloured and the barbel won't be feeding. It all ties up, doesn't it?

If you do find conditions right, you won't need much groundbait and you shouldn't have much difficulty in placing what you do use, correctly. If you have plenty of worms—and mild damp autumn nights are the best times of all for collecting lobs—you can't do better than put some into clay cups with clay lids stuck on, and then lower them gently into the right place, on the end of a shotted line. You can jerk this clear when the clay cup is on the bottom.

Unless you're fishing a very slack place—and more barbel are in slacks than most anglers suppose—don't throw in loose worms. They'll end up miles downstream. Make sure they're where they'll do some good, and if you can't be sure, don't put any in at all.

I want to emphasize this point about barbel coming close to the bank in the right conditions of weather and water, because I see so many anglers casting legers halfway across the river at times when they'd do better to drop their baits 2 or 3ft out from the bank. If there is a clear run under the bank from which you're fishing and the water carries enough colour to prevent your seeing the bottom of it, fish it. Don't be afraid to do so, even if it's no more than 18in deep. The biggest barbel that ever swam doesn't measure 18in from back to belly, so he can easily move into that depth of water.

Bankside runs

If a small rise of level after a warmish night has put a nice lot of worms into the water, and you've added to their numbers by clay-cup groundbaiting, well it'd be a funny thing if the barbel didn't move in to take advantage, wouldn't it?

Some years ago, I used to catch barbel from the Kennet by fishing these bankside runs in the right conditions. I used a 6ft split-cane rod weighing 2½oz, because there was only a narrow space between the river edge and a barbed wire fence, and with a longer rod it was difficult to fish sufficiently close in.

That should give you some idea of how close in barbel will come when the state of the water suits them; and of course the closer in you can fish, the less bother you encounter from dead leaves and weed.

27 The pike

The pike is the subject of more legends, lies, exciting true stories, and dreadful misconceptions than any other freshwater species. So let us first lay down a few facts.

Pike can grow to very great size and I would not discount the possibility of weights as high as 70 or 80lb. The biggest fish are likely to be found in waters that not only produce large numbers of good-sized non-migratory fish, but also have a run of migratory species which put on weight in the sea, thus bringing in additional nutrition to what the loch or lake itself produces.

For example, Loch Lomond, as well as having its own thriving populations of roach, perch, powan, brown trout, and eels, also has a run of salmon and sea-trout, as well as flounders that come in from the sea.

In ancient times, pike populations were kept in balance by such predators as otters, ospreys, and sea-eagles, but these creatures are now reduced in numbers to a considerable degree. Otters are far less numerous, ospreys are reduced to a few pairs, and sea-eagles are extinct in Britain.

Few people realize how heavy this natural predation on pike used to be. Observations at Loch Garten have shown that a single pair of ospreys, during the period between hatching their eggs and the time when the young birds start catching their own fish, catch and consume about 500lb of pike, the pike being their main food. With such predators removed, it is not surprising that on many waters, pike populations can easily get out of hand.

Lately, a great deal of criticism has been made of anglers who have killed one or two pike. Clearly, indiscriminate slaughter of pike is undesirable. Equally, failure to cull pike to some extent must result in an unnatural state of affairs in a fishery.

The pike is a predatory scavenger. It will eat fish of any kind, including its own, alive or dead. It will eat any kind of waterfowl it can swallow, it will eat rats, mice, frogs, newts. It has a preference for prey of a particular size; the bigger the pike, the bigger the fish or other animal it likes to eat.

It can detect its prey by scent, sight, or the detection of vibration, and in the last respect it is specially well equipped. I am convinced that a pike can tell what other fish are swimming about, over a very large area indeed—perhaps as much as a mile. It can certainly detect the presence of a dead fish that is stongly scented, such as a herring or mackerel, at a distance of several hundred yards, which is why a combination of a patient angler and a dead bait is so often successful.

Unless you drop your dead bait close to a pike, you have to allow time for the scent of the bait to reach the pike, and more time for the pike to locate the source of that scent. But you can be fairly sure that both things will happen if you wait long enough.

There is no kind of water a pike won't live in, provided it is not polluted, but there is a very great difference between the

112

strength and fighting qualities of pike in different waters. I'd be happy to tackle any pike in rivers and lakes in the Midlands and the South of England, or on the Norfolk Broads, with a carp rod and a 10 or 12lb line. On a water like Loch Lomond, I'd need a rod at least twice as powerful and a line at least twice as strong, to give me the same chance of landing a pike of equal weight.

Don't take my word alone for it. Bill Giles, who is certainly one of the best pike fishers alive, and some would unhesitatingly call him the best, told me that Loch Lomond pike were three times as powerful as those of the Broads. Pete Thomas, one of the few people who have caught pike, carp, and salmon over 20lb, also regards Lomond pike as three times as powerful as those of the South and Midlands, so remember this if you seek pike in the big waters of Scotland or Ireland.

Pike don't like to lie in fast water, but in quick rivers they'll shoot out into the fast water to grab a bait. They tend to lie near the banks, and anglers waste a lot of time and effort covering the mid-stream area. In lakes, pike may be found almost anywhere, but a scented bait will bring them to you, and you don't need to spend so much time seeking them. On slow rivers, pike congregate in some places. Find one and you may pull several good fish out of it.

Victorian anglers used to think that the colder the weather, the better the chances of catching pike. We now know that the milder winter days are better, but it is true to say that it is never so cold that the chances of catching pike are nil. As with perch, winter sunshine increases anglers' chances.

A few years ago, I'd have said that fishing for pike after dark was largely a waste of time. Now I'm not so sure, having caught quite a few in the night on dead baits intended for eels. I don't, however, think that night fishing offers any advantages.

As everyone knows, the pike has a huge mouth containing hundreds of teeth and very little flesh or membrane into which a hook can be easily stuck. For that reason, it is desirable to use hooks with short sharp points and small barbs.

It is now fashionable to use large landing nets in pike fishing. I am not at all sure that this is wise, since it often involves a dreadful tangle of net mesh, pike teeth, and treble hooks. A skilfully used gaff applied under a pike's chin causes minimal damage and my friends and I have often caught pike that we gaffed and released only a day or two before.

Little pike dash off in alarm if they see you on the bank, but bigger ones are not easily scared by seeing you, though a sudden thump on the bank or bottom of the boat will alarm pike of all sizes.

As well as showing a preference for a particular size of prey related to the size of the pike, pike also have decided preferences for certain species of fish, and I have no doubt whatever that the best possible pike bait is a trout. Next to that, a grayling. Time after time I have seen dead baits such as roach, dace, bream, and chub lie for hours without being taken. Then a dead trout has been cast out and within a minute or two, it has been taken by a pike. Next to trout and grayling comes mackerel, followed by herrings. Though on a lake or loch that contains white fish, such as powan, I think these fish would equal trout, if they could be obtained.

Another excellent bait is a small pike. I catch quite a few by accident from trout waters, and I take them all home to freeze for pike baits. And although pike often seem to vary their preference from day to day in respect to the colour scheme and action of artificial lures such as plugs and spoons, the colour scheme that I have found successful most often is one that imitates a baby pike—olive-green back, white belly, and silvery sides with diagonal primrose-yellow bars.

Which reminds me—there's a rare colour variation in pike. Twice in my life I've caught a pike that had a blue back, brilliant silver sides, a white belly—chalk white, not yellowish—and brilliant crimson fins and tail. A most beautiful and spectacular fish.

In dealing with pike in this series, I am more acutely conscious than with any other species of the limitations of space. So may I add that if you want to know more consult Fred Buller's monumental book, *Pike*, published by MacDonalds, which is the best book about a single species of fish that has ever been written.

28 Persuade pike to come to you

The most important thing in successful fishing is locating your fish. Usually, this means finding where the fish are, but not always. Sometimes it can have the more positive meaning, of bringing fish where you want them to be. With some species, this is seldom possible. For example, bream usually move along well established routes, and to catch them you have to place both your groundbait and hook-bait on the route.

Some other species are more accommodating. For example, you can collect shoals of rudd almost anywhere you like by anchoring crusts. You can clear an open space in a weedbed and attract tench into it, provided you choose the right conditions of light in relation to the depth of the water.

Clarifying

What about pike? Dr Rickards says I am wrong to say that you don't have to cast long distance to catch pike. This is something that needs clarifying.

I don't and didn't mean that pike are always within 10yd of the bank. Of course, they may often be far out in a river or lake. In deep lakes, weather conditions may drive them into deeper water, and that is usually well out from the banks.

There are also circumstances where the pike follows fish on which they prey. If those fish are far out, the pike will be far out also. I am the last to suggest that learning to cast a long way is of no benefit. On the contrary, I have always advocated learning to cast a long way, whether with fly-fishing equipment, coarse fishing tackle, spinning tackle, or the gear you use for fishing dead baits for pike.

As far as my own fishing goes, however, I never cast a yard farther than is necessary, and most of the fish I catch are hooked at quite modest distances. The long throw is only made when there is no alternative, and the reasons are obvious. The shorter the range, the easier it is to detect a bite, and the better are the chances of hooking and landing the fish.

Vibrations

I said earlier that one reason why pike might be a long way from the bank is that they follow the fish on which they prey. They detect these fish in various ways, among which are the detection of vibrations caused by the swimming action of the food fish, and also by scent. Consequently, the angler can often, I might even say usually, attract pike to where he would like them to be, rather than go to the trouble of casting great distances with the accompanying handicaps which that imposes.

Some years ago, I read a most interesting article by Barrie Rickards, in which he described how, as part of a scientific experiment, he had trapped pike in narrow drains—ditches, in fact—a long way from the river. If my memory is not at fault, these pike had run a hundred yards or more up the ditch. Why? Because Barrie had baited the traps. I think the bait was herring; at any rate, it was a kind of fish that was fairly strongly scented.

Now, if the scent of a fish will attract pike long distances up ditches, who needs to cast long distances? All you have to do is drop your dead bait into the water, and in time, the pike will find it.

There may be circumstances in which they take a long time to find it. They may even take longer than you have time to wait. But leave a dead fish on the bottom of any water holding pike, and sooner or later, a pike will arrive and chomp it—if eels don't get it first.

I said earlier that pike can detect their prey through vibrations caused by the prey swimming. Few people agree with me when I say that pike can sense vibrations at great distances, but I believe it firmly. To take an example, I think the pike in Loch Lomond know where all the shoals of powan are within a radius of a mile, and they know by detecting vibrations. Water is a far better conductor of sound than air, yet we can hear sound in air at great distances.

So if you want pike close to where you are fishing, you need prey fish close, and that isn't very difficult to arrange. How often has a pike invaded a swim that you've worked up with groundbait for roach, dace, or bream, specially in a match? As these fish twist and turn among the groundbait, they produce vibrations that pike can detect at great distances—and they 'home' on these vibrations.

116

Consequently, the pike fisher has two ways of bringing pike close in: he can use a dead bait with an attractive scent (or an attractive smell if you prefer that word) and, as an alternative, he can use groundbait that will attract small fish and set them moving actively that way.

Attracts

He can also cast out a vibrating artificial such as a spoon, and keep on casting and retrieving this close to his dead bait. That often attracts pike, which may attack either the artificial or the dead bait.

Usually, if pike aren't fairly near the banks when you start fishing, there is a choice of ways of attracting them there. But often enough, the pike are near the banks anyway. In rivers especially, since pike are not very keen on working against strong currents. You therefore find them where the current is slow, or even completely slack, and such places are usually near the banks.

Where a lot of match fishing is done, the pike soon learn that after the weigh-in, they are going to have a wonderful nósh-up, when the catches are returned. Some of these returned fish are dead, others are in poor shape, and even those least affected by capture and retention in a keep-net are relatively easy for the pike to chomp. Sometimes the pike are so impatient to get at these fish that they don't wait for them to be tipped out of the keep-nets, they actually attack the keep-nets. Anyone who was fished in more than three or four matches will have seen this happen, either to his own net or to that of another competitor pegged close by.

In still waters, pike are less likely to be close in, but they can usually be attracted, if you go the right way about that. That there are exceptions, I do not deny. What is important is the realization that they are exceptions. On most days, either the pike are close in or can be attracted close in.

It is easy to form the impression that long casts of 60 or 70yd are important in pike fishing. An angler who believes this is so will make long casts, and his herring or mackerel will attract pike. The bait is taken, and the angler says 'There you are, that proves that long casting catches you pike!' In most cases, if that

117

angler had used a second rod to cast a similar bait no more than 10yd, he would have found that the short range bait produced more runs, and that he hooked firmly a higher percentage of taking fish.

By all means choose equipment that is capable of long casting, and learn to use it properly. But you will catch more pike at short range, on most days, if you only give yourself the chance to do so.

29 Carp—how to catch 'em

With the opening of the 1970 coarse fishing season, the thoughts of many anglers will be focused on catching carp. So this week I am going to talk about some of the carp fishing problems that crop up most often in the letters which I receive from readers.

First, there is the matter of deciding whereabouts, in any carp water, to start fishing. This can only be solved by doing a lot of watching, to see where the carp feed. The best time for this is early in the morning, in calm weather. Then you can see the bubbles sent up by feeding fish. If there are rush-beds you will usually find carp quite near to them, and they also like to be near fallen trees in the water, which poses problems in the matter of tackle strength.

Then there is the question of the best time to fish. It is a fallacy that carp can only be caught in the dark. Years ago, we did a lot of night fishing because that was the time when there was least disturbance. Nowadays, some carp waters are subject to the attentions of people who cause so much disturbance at night, what with stamping about the banks, lighting fires, using powerful lamps, and so on, that it might be better to fish at midday. Even in the 1950s though, my carp fishing friends and I caught more carp in daylight than we did in the dark.

By all means fish at night, but don't imagine that that is the only time when you can catch big carp, or that night fishing will solve all your problems. Another problem is very soft mud or weed cover on the bottom. Balanced paste and crust bait solves this in most cases. You put a bit of crust on the bend of your hook, and mould enough paste around the shank, up against the crust, to make the combined bait just, and only just, sink.

You can do much the same thing with boiled potatoes. Cut a bit off the potato so as to leave a flat surface; thread the line through the potato so that it emerges from the centre of the flat surface. Then tie on the hook, stick a bit of crust on it, and slide the potato down until its flat surface is up against the crust. That not only slows down the sinking rate; it also prevents the potato being thrown off the hook by the force of the cast. In turn this allows you to use softer potatoes, which I am sure carp prefer to partially boiled ones.

Of course there are many other ways of dealing with soft or bottom weed. You can attach a lead by means of a link of nylon made as long as the weed or mud is deep, and ending in a small swivel through which your main line passes. A shot or nylon stop prevents the swivel from running down to the hook. You can also use a wooden casting weight, loaded with enough lead to make it only just sink. If you make it from greenheart, you won't use much lead. Some samples of greenheart sink without any lead at all.

Now for the matter of bites. If you get a positive run, with the line peeling away off your reel, there is no problem. You engage the reel pick-up, wait until the line tightens, then strike firmly. The farther you cast, the harder you have to strike. With a fibreglass rod, wait until you feel the fish before you strike. You won't connect with every run, because there are times when carp pick up a bait between their lips, very cunningly, and run off with it without the hook ever being in their mouths.

When you strike, you miss

Delaying the strike gets you nowhere, because if you wait the carp drops the bait. There is not a thing you can do about this, and what makes it even more maddening is that when carp decide to play this game they keep at it.

You may get up to twenty apparently good runs at a sitting, and miss every one. If you do hook any fish it is usually at the root of one of its pectoral fins. Chub, tench, and bream sometimes play this game. A change of bait, or a smaller bait, may get you a fish when it is going on, but not often.

Now what about 'twitch' bites

The simple answer is that you strike when you are reasonably sure that a biting fish has the bait in its mouth. Carp don't always run off with your bait. They may pick it up and go on feeding in the same place, especially in the groundbaited area. If the movement of your line seems to indicate that this has happened, then strike.

But be careful. A lot of other things may cause little pulls and twitches in your line. Small fish may be pushing your bait about. Swirls and vortices of water produced by big fish moving near your line may make it move a good deal. If you strike at every line movement, you'll end up by scaring the carp and spoiling your chances.

So you've got to use judgement

If you are in doubt, try tightening gently. If you feel the sort of resistance you expect if a carp had your bait in his mouth, then give him a solid dig.

Such problems vanish if you decide to use the surface bait like floating crusts. That doesn't succeed on all carp water, by any means; but where it does it can be deadly. Especially if it takes the form of margin fishing, which is fishing a floating crust right under the rod point, With none of the line touching the water at all.

Use a multiplier or a centre-pin if you like. If you use a fixed spool, leave the pick-up engaged but have a couple of feet of slack line between butt ring and reel, so that a taking fish can get his head down before the line comes tight. Otherwise, a carp will suck the wet crust straight off the hook.

The most important thing about margin fishing is to stay perfectly still and quiet for hours at a time. Getting up and stretching, wandering about, flashing lights, and so on, will entirely spoil your chances.

Finally, do make sure that all your gear is sound. Test your line and hook—which should be kept deadly sharp. Make sure your reel is in first class order and that its slipping clutch or star drag is correctly set—remembering that with some reels, clutch-setting can tighten up if the temperature falls, which is normally after sundown.

In spite of tremendous improvement in tackle, tactics, and general knowledge, carp fishing still means fewer bites per hour of fishing than in any other branch of angling. You don't want to miss chances through failing to check up on every detail before starting to fish.

30 Tactics to catch the lovely rudd

Several readers have asked for an article about rudd fishing so here it is!

You've only got to look at a rudd's mouth to see that it is mainly a surface-feeder, and that tells you a lot about rudd fishing. Except when the weather is cold, you can expect to catch rudd near the surface and in shallow water. You can also expect to find these fish where there is surface weed, lily-pads, or beds of reeds. Rudd like to pick snails and water insects from these plants, and on some waters the shoals can be spotted by the way in which lily-pads are lifted or reeds are agitated.

Fixing a float

The traditional, and still perhaps the most effective method of fishing for rudd is by casting float tackle at long range. Modern fixed-spool reels and monofil lines have greatly increased the effectiveness of this technique, while the modern long hollow, fibreglass or aluminium alloy rods, help striking at long distances.

When fishing only a foot or 18in below the float, however, it is necessary to take steps to avoid the hook getting caught over the top of the float; a piece of rubber tubing, through which the line is threaded, pushed only partly on the float top, helps to avoid this trouble. Many rudd fishers favour self-cocking floats; a piece of clean swan quill with a wooden plug makes an excellent rudd float, as the right number of shot can be inserted before the plug is fitted and held in place with a bit of balsa-wood and cellulose varnish. Any float will serve, however, provided it can be seen at long range. Extreme sensitivity is not necessary, as a feeding rudd will drag quite heavy float tackle a long way without taking fright at the resistance it must surely feel.

Rudd can often be induced to feed at the surface by throwing or drifting bread crust out to them. The ordinary long-range float tackle will usually catch them then, the bait being maggot, paste, or worm; but occasionally they will insist on taking only a bait that actually floats. Then you have to give them floating crust cubes, and in order to have weight enough for casting, you can use a fairly heavy self-cocking float, attached by threading the line through the cap, down through the bottom ring, and then back through the cap so that both the reel line and the hook length come out at the top. The float turns over on the bite.

In shallow water, rudd can be caught by means of the lift method used at long range, with crust cubes as bait; or if the bottom is not too soft, you can use ordinary float-legering or laying-on methods to fish with such baits as maggots, paste, worm, or wormtail, all of which are good rudd baits.

Leger a crust

While float-fishing is usually best, a strong wind can make it awkward to use, and then a straightforward leger often succeeds, especially with a crust cube bait and the lead only a few inches from the hook. It is, however, tricky to fish so from a boat, and for that it may be better to use a float leger with the float attached by its bottom end and the line well sunk, putting a dust shot or two on the line above the float to ensure this.

One little known fact about rudd is that they have predatory tendencies, and can sometimes be caught on a tiny fly-spoon or devon minnow, spun as one would for trout or perch. They have a decided preference for gilt, and I have often had small ones take a bare gilt hook. Being keen insect eaters, rudd can also be caught by fly-fishing. They will take almost any kind of fly, from a big, bushy-bodied white moth floated on the surface to a wet Wickham's Fancy, sunk and retrieved in slow pulls. For big rudd, my favourite hook size is No 10 whether fly- or bait-fishing.

In colder weather, rudd shoals swim deeper and one has to search for the taking depth. The fish occasionally make for deeper water in very hot weather too, especially in the early morning, while in winter they can sometimes be caught with float tackle that has the shot anything from 6in to 3ft from the hook, which is baited with crust to float above the shot. By varying the distance between hook and shot, the distance that suits the fish can generally be found.

One more method, which accounts for specimen rudd even though it seldom makes a big catch in numbers, is margin fishing, using exactly the same technique as is used for carp but with smaller hooks and baits, and finer line—4lb bs is usually strong enough. There is little advantage in fishing finer, as rudd are not at all tackle shy. They are, however, wary of a snaky shadow cast on the bottom by a floating line, and in such circumstances as cause this effect the line must be sunk, at least the 3 or 4yd nearer the float.

Cast to weeds

The approach varies with the water concerned; on large lakes and on the Broads, a boat is a great help. It can be anchored 30 or 40yd from the fish; in many lakes this means anchoring well out and casting towards the edges of beds of weeds or broad patches of rushes, reeds or lily-pads.

Fishing from the bank is often more difficult; but don't be afraid to cast out over the weeds or lilies. If your float is attached by rubber tubes at top and bottom it will come through safely nine times out of ten, and so will the rudd you hook.

Few big fish

The rudd is one of Britain's (and Ireland's) most beautiful fish, very much worth pursuing. It is also perhaps, the least likely species to produce a new record, very few anglers having come near the Rev E C Alston's fish of 4½lb which he caught from Ring Mere in Norfolk in 1933. Even a fish of half the record weight is a very creditable catch and if you get half a dozen between 1½lb and 2½lb you will have a grand catch.

Perhaps it may include a rare yellow-finned specimen with banana coloured under fins. They do exist, and I've got a colour picture of a brace of two-pounders, one with yellow and one with the usual red fins, that Fred J Taylor caught, to prove it.

31 The lift lures fat old tench

An angling writer in a provincial evening paper recently described the lift method, during which he made this remarkable statement: 'If you tackle up correctly, the float will be lying on the top of the water and will stand upright when you get a bite.' I can only suppose this is a printer's error, but since a reader has written to me, sending a cutting, I feel there must be many readers who don't understand the lift method, so for their benefit I'll describe it.

Basic method

Basically, it consists simply of having the shot very close to the hook and adjusting the tackle so that the float is nicely cocked when the shot is touching bottom. A fish picking up the bait must lift the shot, and then the float rises or 'lifts'. If the fish lifts the shot enough, the float topples over and lies flat.

This method has been in use for at least half a century and I remember my grandfather using it on the Lea when I was a small boy. The credit for developing and publicizing it, however, goes to the Taylor brothers of Aylesbury, who have made fabulous catches of tench with it.

Experience in using it taught that the best way to fish it was with the float attached by the bottom end only and set about 30 per cent further from the shot than the depth of the swim. The tackle is cast out, when of course the float lies flat. The rod is then put in a rest and line is wound in until the float cocks with just the right amount of top showing above the surface. This prevents the line from rising vertically above the shot.

Beginners note—when using the lift method, the rod *must* be in a rest. You can't hold it in your hand because if you do, the float will be continually bobbing about due to the unavoidable movement of your hand. This method is incredibly sensitive, both to bites and to rod movement, so you minimize the latter by using a rest.

For tench fishing, the favourite float is a piece of peacock quill, which should be cut to suit the shot, so that it just fails to

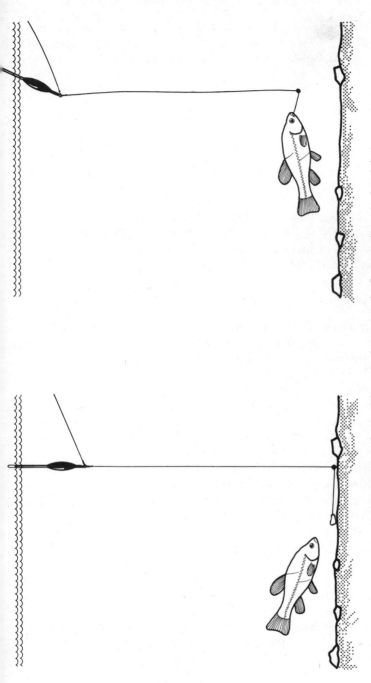

(*left*) A tackle rig for the lift method showing the float nicely cocked with bait and shot on the bottom; (*right*) as the fish picks up the bait and displaces the weight of the shot, the float will rise out of the water with a pronounced 'lift'

go under when carrying the full weight of the shot. There are conditions which demand an even more sensitive variation of the 'lift' though. With the ordinary peacock quill, or any other quill for that matter, when the fish lifts the shot, he can feel its weight more and more as the float rises, until, when the float is flat, he is carrying the full weight of the shot.

Normally, a fat old tench isn't bothered by this, but in a heavily fished water it can make a tench that has been caught once or twice before, take alarm and spit the bait out. And when the method is used for big roach, this shot weight can sometimes really spoil your chances. I found this happening when after some very big and very shy roach, so I devised a way of avoiding the trouble, which I've told you about before. It consists simply of fishing with the float well under water, using enough shot just, but only just, to sink it, and then having an antenna stuck in the float that reaches to the surface.

Bread bait

With this, the float is carrying 99.99 per cent of the weight of the shot and continues to do so when a fish 'lifts' until the float proper (not counting the antenna) has reached the surface.

These, then, are the ways in which you can use the 'lift' method, and a very useful method it is. It is usually used with bread crust as bait, but of course other baits can also be used. Remember that with crust you must take account of the buoyancy of the bait itself. If you change your bait size, you will have to adjust your shotting accordingly.

Essentially, the 'lift' is a stillwater method, but it can be used in slow rivers and canals with a 'draw', provided the current isn't too fast. Not only is it very effective; it is also one of those ways of angling that is fascinating to use. If everything is correct, there sits your float top, absolutely motionless.

Needle-bubbles come up here and there in your baited pitch and you watch as they come nearer and nearer to your float. Suddenly, it grows. That's the only way to describe it—it's like some fantastic plant shoot getting longer before your very eyes.

Sometimes it grows slowly; sometimes it fairly shoots up out of the water. You can never be quite sure what fish is causing its antics, but you learn that more often than not, the slower the rise, the bigger the fish.

Strike carefully

Once in a blue moon, instead of lifting, the float suddenly disappears. Watch how you strike when it does, because this is a fish that has taken the bait and made off very fast and straight away from you. It may be a baby rudd, but equally it may be a specimen tench and if you hammer him too hard, you'll break.

One last point, if the surface of the water is choppy, fish the 'lift' with an antenna float and set your rod in two rests, the rear rest high, so your rod point is touching the surface of the water. Then you won't be troubled by wind and drift.

32 How to catch those big perch

Now is the time for those anglers who fish deep lakes and reservoirs to start thinking about catching big perch. With cooler conditions, the large perch gather together in shoals and move into deeper water, and after a few sharp night frosts most of them will be in the deepest holes they can find.

The sort of day I have found most productive for these deep water perch is that following a clear, cold night that has put a cat-ice round the fringes of the lake, ice that disappears as the sun gains strength. I've always done best on sunny days, perhaps because there is more light in the depths.

I don't need to describe at length the method used to catch big perch in deep water, because I expect most readers know it by now.

Your tackle

Briefly, you need a flexible casting rod, a fixed-spool reel, some Arlesey bombs, and some eyed hooks. I use a 6lb line, 1oz bombs, and a No 6 hook. The bait is lobworms.

You find your deepest hole by casting experimentally and noting the time the lead takes to sink, and you check your direction by watching various landmarks on the opposite bank.

That much, most people know, but there are many ways in which an angler can spoil his chances. I've seen so many visitors at Arlesey lake who could have caught perch but instead threw away their chances, that I think it may help more if I say what should be avoided than if I repeat what should be done.

Best spot

First of all, don't think that what matters is where you stand. At Arlesey, and I expect in other waters, you'll find out easily enough where anglers stood when they caught big perch. Not only the locals but the beaten ground will tell you the favourite spots. Just standing there and casting at random won't do you a bit of good. You must do your own depth testing, unless you've been there before and know the mark already.

Having found your deepest place, make sure you cast there every time. Don't be content to let an off-line cast lie. Pull it up and cast again, and again if necessary, till your bait is where you want it. Then be methodical. Move it in, say 20yd, re-cast and begin again. Or you can use two rods, one bait cast into the deep, and the other on the left or right, in slightly shallower water. Work one in, re-cast, and then work in the other. Don't just cast out and let the bait lie all day, hoping a perch will find it. Keep on searching, and use a fresh worm for every cast.

Lost chance

Don't use dough-bobbins or any other bite indicator that offers a check to a running fish. I've seen literally dozens of chances lost that way. Use something that will free the line when the pull comes, so the fish can run without check—and let him run 5yd at least, before you hit him.

When you do hit him, make no mistake about it. Half-hearted striking loses more perch than anything. Take a yard of 6lb nylon line and stretch it between your hands. It gives 3in or more, doesn't it? So if you've cast 70yd, there will be three times 70in of stretch to take up on the strike—17ft!

128

Line sag

Then there will be several more feet of sag in the line, on top of which your biting perch may have run yards, straight towards you. So, on the bite, take a good sweep back over your shoulder, or sideways; step back as many paces as you need to feel the fish, and strike again. Don't be afraid you'll break at the strike; if your tackle is sound, you couldn't break if you tried, except by pointing the rod straight down the line and walking ten or more yards backwards.

In snagless waters, all that remains is to play your fish in your own time. At Arlesey, and in many other lakes and reservoirs, there are bad snags, and when your perch is struck you must go to work to pump him up off the bottom. Don't wait for him to make the moves; his first one will be into a sunken tree, or, at Arlesey, round a steel cable, a truck, or into a shed 30ft down. So fetch your fish up without any delay. You won't break with lots of line out, its stretch absorbs the jerks and jags of the fish.

When your big perch is safely landed, make up your mind right away whether you are going to kill him or let him go. If he's come up from 20ft or more, you can't as a rule keep him in a keep-net. Perch can't adjust the pressure in their swim-bladders quickly, and if you put your big chap in a keep-net, within ten or fifteen minutes he'll be on his back, with a blown-out tummy, and unable to swim right way up, let alone get down to deep water again. Eventually, he'll die.

Only way

The only way of keeping such fish alive is to put them into a keep-net that can be sunk, with its neck tied up, into deep water right away, and even then, continually pulling it up for more fish to go in—if you keep on catching them—will probably kill those first put into it.

My advice is to weigh your fish quickly and let him go, unless you want him for a glass case.

33 Grayling

Few species of fish can be caught by such a variety of methods as the grayling. You can catch them on dry-fly, wet-fly, nymph, and small lure. You can catch them by trotting with float tackle, by legering, or on a paternoster. You can sometimes catch them by spinning, with a tiny spoon or a devon minnow.

When I go grayling fishing, I always take two outfits: a light fly rod carrying a No 5 line and a 12ft match type rod, which can be used for trotting or legering. If I find the grayling rising, I fit up the fly rod, with a leader 9ft long tapered to 2lb. I try to identify the insects on which the grayling are feeding, I tie on an imitation, and waterproof it with Permaflote. If I can't catch fish with that, I usually try a small nymph, fished just below the surface; and if that fails, I may give a brief trial to a fancy fly such as a Red Tag.

There are times when rising grayling can be absolutely maddening, rising steadily at what the Americans call 'No-see-ums', and refusing to take any fly you can offer. I don't know the answer to this. You can try a very tiny fly, size 22, attached to a 1lb bs leader point, and perhaps hook a fish or two, breaking at the strike on some, losing some in the weed, and having some come off the hook.

Leaded shrimp

If the grayling are not rising, but I can see them, I usually try them with a leaded nymph or a leaded shrimp. If they're in water no deeper than a couple of feet, I try a leaded or copper-wire-loaded nymph, Pheasant Tail, Hare's Ear, or Olive feather fibre. If they're a bit too deep then I try a small leaded shrimp or a Mead Mill Special. If these won't go deep enough, I put on a bigger leaded shrimp.

You can make any weighted fly fish deeper by casting across the current, and directly the line falls on the water, switching upstream to produce an upstream curve. The fly will go on sinking until the current has turned this upstream curve (or 'mend') into a downstream one; then the fly gets pulled up again, and it is then that the take usually comes.

If no grayling are rising, and I can't see any, I usually fix up the float tackle, using 3lb line and a No 14 hook. I should explain here that I do not believe it is necessary to use tiny hooks or ultrafine line to catch grayling, except when imitating very small flies. I do fine with size 14 hooks and 3lb line, and I'm sure far fewer grayling come adrift than if I used 16s and 18s. For more than three hundred years, writers have talked about tender-mouthed grayling, probably because grayling have tough mouths, into which it needs force to stick a hook. You can't apply much force with very fine lines.

Grayling, traditionally, take maggots or small worms, and these, being easy to get, I usually use. But grayling will also take bread paste, flake, casters, crust cubes, and cheese paste.

There's nothing special about trotting for grayling, except that they're often more willing to come up for a bait fished well off the bottom than are roach or bream. How far they'll come depends, I think, on water temperatures.

If you're loose-feeding with maggots, you must watch your fishing depth all the time, because fish that began by feeding close to the bottom may start rising higher in the water as your loose-feeding goes on.

Balsa float

I suppose I ought to produce a learned screed about what float to use, but I generally use a bird quill of one sort or another. Reg Righyni's balsa float, with a wire stem, is very good; the main thing is to choose a float with its buoyancy balanced nearer the top than the bottom.

In cold conditions, if you can't catch grayling on float tackle, you should try legering. Very few grayling fishers ever try it, and you'll find nothing about it in books about grayling fishing. It involves nothing very special; you fix up a swan-shot leger and fish it in the slacker water. Regular readers will know that I detect bites by touch, but if you're too idle to learn that, you can use a swing or a quiver tip.

Baits can be maggots, small worms, or the tail-ends of bigger worms, but on some waters you may find bootlace eels a nuisance. They certainly are on the Test and parts of the Avon. In that case, use bread crust cubes, about the size of a pea when dry, or pinches of new bread flake. These are baits you will not

131

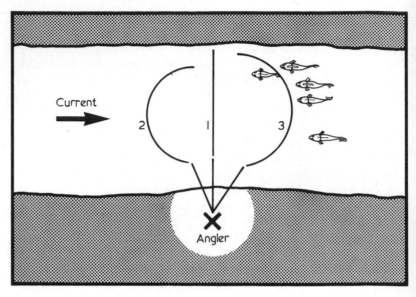

Fishing the leaded shrimp for grayling: 1—cast straight across; 2—mend line upstream, keep rod still and let current pull line to 3

see mentioned in books about grayling, but grayling do in fact take bread baits.

Sometimes you can catch plenty of grayling by fishing a leaded artificial shrimp on a float tackle. The secret is to keep checking the float strongly, so as to make the shrimp rise in the water. You let the float run a couple of feet, then check it for five seconds or so, then let it run another 2ft and so on.

The paternoster can sometimes prove effective. You tie a Double Grinner knot in your line, leaving one end about 4in long and the other a foot or more. Tie a knot in this end and pinch on a bunch of swan-shot, all touching, as many as is necessary to hold bottom. On the short end, tie a hook, or a leaded shrimp. If you use a hook, bait it with a fat maggot. Cast, and when the shot reach bottom, move the rod top slowly up and down. This will make the bait, or the artificial shrimp, rise and fall in the water. You cannot do this very well with a swing or a quiver tip, so you'll have to feel for bites.

Well, there you have a variety of baits, flies, and methods, and on most days, one or another will catch you some grayling.

There are, however, days when grayling are practically impossible to catch. In my experience, if a chalk stream is running coloured, even slightly, grayling are going to be very difficult to tempt; and if as well as being coloured, the water in streams of this sort is cold, below about 40°F, you may as well not bother. I've known more than one day on the Test where such conditions were encountered, and top class anglers failed to touch a single fish.

34 If you want to catch big dace . . .

Several readers have asked me to write something about specimen dace. How big a dace has to be before it can be classed as a specimen I'm not quite sure, but if you want to catch a dace over a pound in weight, the really important thing to do is to choose the right river to fish in.

Dace of that size are rare in any river, but in most rivers they are, for practical purposes, non-existent. I don't mean that there isn't a single 1lb dace in, say, the Thames, or the Ouse, or the Severn. But on such rivers they are so few and far between that it is impossible to plan to catch one.

You could be the world's best dace angler and fish the Thames for a lifetime, and yet never see a 1lb dace. Even on the Hampshire Avon, dace of that size are caught very seldom indeed. The fact is, the dace isn't very fussy about where it will manage to live, but it's very fussy indeed about what sort of water it needs to grow really big. In fact, the only rivers I know in which an angler stands a reasonable chance of catching a dace over a pound are in Hertfordshire and in Suffolk.

I was tempted to include the Kennet, from which quite a number of pounders have been taken, including four in a single season taken by that wonderful angler H T Sheringham. But even on the Kennet, dace of a pound are pretty rare. (I expect some readers will know of rivers where monster dace are not uncommon; I know two.)

One of them is strictly preserved, and permits for most of its length are impossible to obtain. Yet it is a perfect example of the sort of water in which dace grow to specimen size. Fishing in parts of it where the occasional fishing permit is given, I have managed to catch four dace over the pound and up to 1lb 3oz. I've also caught quite a few that ought to have been a pound, and would have been if they'd only eaten a bit more groundbait before I caught them. The noticeable thing about these bigger dace is that they do not behave in the way that most fishing writers say dace do.

I've never caught a big dace in that river or any other with a bait that wasn't either dead on the bottom or floating on the top. And when I say on the bottom, I mean lying still on the bottom. I don't mean to say that big dace can't be caught by long-trotting methods. No doubt they have been so caught. I've caught hundreds and hundreds of ordinary-sized dace that way, but never one over about 10 to 12oz.

Deliberate bite

Another thing about these big dace is that they don't need the greased-lightning strike that we're so often told is necessary to hook dace. I remember once leaving my rod to fish for itself while I went upstream to try to catch some caddis grubs for bait. Pete Thomas, who was with me, called out that I'd got a bite. It took me quite a time to get back to my rod; in fact I arrived just in time to save it being pulled in, and to land the fish—a 14oz dace.

All the dace I've caught of that size or bigger have bitten quite deliberately, much more so than roach of similar size in the same waters, and I've missed more big dace when fly-fishing by striking too soon than by leaving it too late.

The last three months of the coarse fishing season are as good a time as any to try for big dace, dace being a species that doesn't mind temperatures being fairly low. At the same time, I should fish much more hopefully in water above 40°F than below that temperature. In winter, fly-fishing is seldom profitable, and I am sure that laying-on is the best all-round method for the big dace.

A lot of fuss is made about baits, but I fancy that if the fish are willing to feed at all, they're just as likely to take a couple of ordinary maggots or a bit of bread paste, flake, or crust as anything more elaborate, though when the water is well coloured, they will often take a worm, and quite a big worm at that.

If a dace of no more than 4oz will take a lobworm, full-size, on a No 4 hook, as they quite often do when I'm chub fishing, I'm sure a dace of a pound would take a good big worm on a hook about No 8 or 10. But I don't think I'd use such a big bait if I were trying deliberately to catch dace. I'd rather choose a medium-sized red worm, or a marshworm, on a No 12, for fishing thick water, and I'd use a No 14 for maggot or bread baits.

While big dace bite quite deliberately, they won't stand feeling much resistance, and you should ignore advice to lay-on with bait, float, and rod tip all in a straight line. With that set-up, you get a good bang all right, but the fish feels the pull of the rod top and spits the bait out instantly, before you can strike. Leave enough slack between the float and the rod so that only the float, and not the rod top, registers the bite. It is probably the same reason that makes dace hard to catch on leger.

35 I'm sure there are 20lb eels

Very few anglers seem interested in eel fishing. Perhaps their experiences with small eels which have been caught accidentally have made them regard all eels as nuisances.

It is true that the unwanted eel can be a great pest, especially if it be a little one. But big eels, fished for intentionally, can provide very good sport and good food, too. One of the advantages of the bigger eels is that you can fish for them with excellent chances of success at times when you would be very lucky indeed to catch a good fish of any other species.

Club anglers have often told me that on coach-outings they have very little chance of coming to grips with specimen fish. The times of arrival and departure at the venue, and the fact that among a coachload of anglers there seems always to be one or two who cannot refrain, if they are getting no bites, from wandering up and down and spoiling everyone else's chances, certainly make the catching of most kinds of fish difficult on these occasions.

The one exception is the eel, and I believe that if anglers who caught big eels were given the credit that is their due, more club men would fish for eels and have plenty of sport with them.

Let others say what they will about eels; I say that a big eel is as creditable a catch as a big fish of any other kind, and it is no mean feat to land one, even on quite strong tackle. Fishing the Wye last week, using cheese paste for chub, I had a terrific bite, struck, and was forthwith connected with what felt like a 6lb chub at least. The fish, landed after quite a struggle, turned out to be an eel of 1½lb.

Dead fish bait

Not only can an eel put up a tremendous fight, but he's a problem to land even when brought to bank. He'll go backwards out of a landing net in no time, and twist off a gaff just as quickly. For anyone who wants to specialize in catching big eels, there's room for inventiveness in devising something with which to land them such as a pair of tongs with toothed jaws or something of that kind. Really big eels have wire-cutting jaws, and somehow continue to bite through even quite stout wire traces, unless you know the trick of preventing it, which is bound up with the matter of the bait used.

The bait I always use is a small dead fish, and here we come up against a bit of a snag for the club angler, because there's sure to be a moan raised by somebody about small fish being killed for eel baits. *The answer is, of course, that every eel caught means saving the lives of hundreds of small fish as well as quantities of spawn.*

The way to use them is to thread the line through from tail to mouth with a baiting-needle, tie a hook to the end and draw it back into the mouth of the bait so that its point lies alongside and outside the bait's check. For big eels a No 4 hook is a useful size. Then attach a piece of matchstick with a clove-hitch, or else pinch on a big split-shot, as close to where the line enters the tail of the bait as possible. When the eel is hooked, he will try to blow out the bait, and if he could do it, he could then close his jaws on the line and proceed to bite through it. But the matchstick or shot prevents the bait being blown out, and as a result the eel is gagged and can't bite the line. You mustn't forget to see that the swim-bladder of your bait is deflated, or else it won't sink.

For stillwater work you won't need lead, as the bait will be heavy enough for casting, but in running water you'll need a lead, which must let the line run through it freely, I use an Arlesey bomb.

Eels hunt by scent, and each eel knows that he is not the only one which has scented the bait. So when he gets to it, he grabs it anyhow and goes off like a shot, just like a chicken with a piece of bread, in case another might take it away from him.

Wait for it

It isn't until he has put some distance between himself and the spot where he found the bait that he stops to swallow it, or at least to begin swallowing it by turning its head into his mouth.

When you get a run, therefore, you must wait till the eel has stopped running and given a few jerks before you strike. It's probably best to wait till he starts off a second time. The whole secret of playing a hooked eel is to get him on the move towards you, and to keep him coming, even if it means running backwards. If he once gets his tail into weeds, or round a snag, you'll have a difficult job shifting him, and may never succeed if he is a really big chap.

And he may very well be a big chap, because there are plenty of them about, in all kinds of waters from big lakes and rivers to tiny farm ponds. The record of $8\frac{1}{2}$lb is nothing like the top weight that could be achieved. *I am sure that eels well over 20lb exist in Britain.* I've seen a dead one of nearly 10lb, but the man who catches one half that size can congratulate himself. He may not receive the praise of every angler, but he can count on mine.

36 Roach, the fish with varying habits

Since it became known that I have caught a few nice-sized roach and dace this season, a lot of readers have written to ask if I have any special methods of catching these fish, or any extra-effective baits that I use. As in the case of other fish, there are no short cuts to success in fishing for roach and dace, but since both are very interesting fish, it might help some of the younger readers if I say a bit about them. I will deal with roach only here as I have already said something about dace.

Before I do, may I say that I regard Edward Ensom ('Fadist') as the leading authority on roach and dace, and no young angler who is interested in these fish should miss reading his book *Roach Fishing*, and his contributions on roach and dace in *Fine Angling for Coarse Fish*. The groundwork is all there. The first thing to realize about roach, as I am sure Ted Ensom would agree, is that no fish varies so much in its habits from one water to another.

Fierce bite

In some waters and in some conditions, roach will bite so fiercely that they'll practically pull the rod in. In other places and in other conditions you have to watch like a hawk and strike at the slightest touch. Generally, it is in heavily fished rivers of moderate pace that the fastest striking is needed; in fast rivers or in still waters you get a more decisive bite. But there are so many exceptions to this that I can only advise the would-be catcher of specimen roach to take the trouble and time to learn the habits of the particular roach he is after and suit his style to those habits.

The 2lb roach I've been catching on a Lea tributary haven't taken the float under yet; I've had to watch carefully and hit the least flicker of the float. Yet, as I said a week or two ago, I've caught 2lb roach that would not only take the float under but the rod point as well if you waited long enough.

The next point is the matter of shoaling. Everyone knows that roach are shoal fish, but what everyone doesn't seem to know is that the type of shoal varies very much in different waters. In some, and especially weedy streams with open runs here and there, you find the fish in any given shoal are much of a size. Some shoals are all fish of 3 to 8oz, others fish of 7 to 14oz, yet others, fish from 1 to 1½lb, and in a good water there will be a few shoals where more of the roach top 2lb than are below that weight.

What you find

This is what you usually find in rivers, where the roach in their shoals have chosen haunts in which they wait for what the current will bring. The amount of moving about done by a roach shoal is least in waters whose current is most rapid, as a rule. Of course, there are plenty of exceptions. I hope everyone realizes by now that as far as I'm concerned, the words never and always have no place in angling!

This 'shoaling by size' habit is important, because knowing about it can save you time. If you try a likely run and catch two or three four-ouncers, it usually (but not always, mind!) means there aren't any specimen roach there. So try somewhere else, and keep on searching till you hit some of the big fellows. When you do find them, you don't have to use big baits to avoid small fish taking them first, because there won't be any small ones in that kind of shoal. This means that where clear water, or a diet of small organisms, have got the roach eating small things, you can use small baits and catch big fish.

When you're searching waters of this kind for the bigger roach, there are several things to remember. One is that the shoals feed at intervals and because you don't get a bite in a likely spot in the first hour or so, don't imagine no roach are there. I'd much rather that happen than catch a few small roach. A swim that looks good but fishes dead often proves to be the one which holds the best roach—and if you try it just before dusk, you may get the glass-case specimen that you've been waiting for.

Next thing is the usual advice about clean gravel bottoms. Roach certainly prefer clean gravel to black mud, but what they really like is a bottom of fine silkweed. Find a nice bottom of good green silkweed, and the chances are roach won't be far off. They eat any amount of silkweed in the summer, and you often catch them oozing it at both ends. Don't let silkweed put you off a likely swim. Fish it so the roach can find your bait despite the silkweed.

Fish fine

Third thing about these shoals is that you scare one and scare the lot; whether it is by letting them see you, by stamping about, by splashy casting, coarse tackle, or tainted bait; put off one and you put off the whole lot. So fish as fine and far off as conditions allow, and take care of the other points as well.

That's one kind of roach shoal. It has its haunt, fish are all much of a size and because you know where they are and where, more or less, they will stay, you don't need much groundbait, just a pinch now and then.

The other kind of roach shoal is the sort that does need groundbait. It is the roving kind of shoal which you find in still waters and big slow rivers without much weed.

Go in shoals

You find it also in many canals, and waters of that type, which have no special features which can form a home for a shoal, and where there is relatively less feed and current to carry the feed; the roach must go in search of it. One of the exceptions in such waters is the silkweed bed. Where these beds are isolated you may find roach constantly in the vicinity, but usually, in these waters, the silkweed is everywhere or nowhere, and the roach shoals move about a lot.

Big ones follow

Whenever shoal-fish move about, groundbait can attract and hold them. Now, unlike the other sorts of water, you shouldn't be discouraged by catching small ones. It shows a shoal of small ones has been attracted, but the big ones may come along later. So fish on, but increase the size of your hook-bait, and throw in a few pieces like the hook-bait every now and then. Fish well down on the bottom, and if necessary because of many small fish about, add extra lead to get down quick.

If all goes well, you'll end up with roach of all sizes in your pitch, and then I advise you (and I am willing to be corrected by expert roach fishers) to wait for the decisive bite and not strike at touches, if it's specimen roach you want.

I am always sorry for reservoir roach anglers who are often forbidden to use groundbait in the very waters which need it most, but as they always seem to catch their share of monster roach, perhaps my sympathy is wasted.

37 Opening-day tench

There's a wide choice of fish with which to start the coarse fishing season, but the kind I prefer is the tench. This week, I've got some advice for readers who agree with me, but who may not know how to get a good tench catch on 16 June.

To begin with, no fish except perhaps the bream, responds as well as the tench to advance preparation. Choose your tench swim at least a week before you intend to fish it, and give the bottom a good dragging with a double-sided rake, if there's little or no weed. If there is much weed, only drag it out if you can groundbait every day. If you can, this will prevent the weed from growing up again. If not, delay the weed removal until the day before you fish, but get a load of groundbait in a week before.

How do you choose a tench swim? Well, the best sort has a gently shelving bottom which allows you to fish at various depths between 2 and 3ft and 8 to 12ft. Try and find one that involves a bed of bulrushes or reeds at one side or the other, preferably both. Tench move into quite shallow water after dark and stay there, until light, except on very cold nights. If your swim lets you start fishing close in, in shallow water, and then move your tackle to deeper and deeper water from dawn onwards, you may keep on getting fish for several hours.

You'll often find that tench move into your swim from one

side or the other, usually through or close alongside reeds or rushes. If you have these plants on one side of your swim, start fishing close to them. If they're on both sides, try casting each way alternately, ten minutes one side, then ten minutes the other, till your first bite tells you which side is the chosen one.

For early-season tench fishing the best all-round bait on most waters is lobworm. Later you may need smaller baits, like maggot, wheat or small worms, but big lobs generally score best in the first week or two of the season. Don't fish them on small hooks or fine line; use a size six on 6lb line.

You don't need a sensitive rig, either. A swan quill float and a swan-shot or two will do nicely. Nor do you need the shot close to the hook. Put it a foot or more away; and don't strike at small movements. Wait until the float sails away positively. If there's a lot of drift, attach your float by the bottom end only and sink the line above it.

A man who wants to catch tench all through the summer, has to be crafty about it. He'll need antenna floats, lift tackles, finer lines, smaller hooks, smaller baits, and all sorts of thing, used to meet changing water conditions and the changing preference of the fish. But for the first couple of weeks of the season none of this finesse is needed. If you can't catch them with simple strong tackle and a good big bait then, you won't catch them at all.

On some waters, tench prefer a big crust or piece of flake to lobworm, so you should have both baits with you, so that if one doesn't attract the fish, you can try the other.

Now and then you may find freshwater mussel does better than either, but that is quite unusual. Still, you will probably know from dragging your swim if there are many mussels about and if there are, it's a good idea to keep a couple of dozen in a net in the water, in case you want to try a bit of mussel when you're fishing. Don't go mad about mussels, though. If you make a good catch with mussel you may be tempted to collect and use them by the hundreds, for outing after outing. It doesn't take many other anglers doing the same thing, to make very serious inroads into the mussel population of a lake, with noticeable effects on the growth rate of the tench.

What about groundbait for tench? The nearer fish get to where you put it in, the more they find, but the groundbait must be widespread or the fish won't be attracted from far away. Ox blood, mixed with light groundbait, increases its attraction for tench, but you must buy it with an anti-coagulant mixed in or your blood will set solid. If you mix it in while still liquid, the groundbait will set like black pudding and fail to spread as it should. You don't really need ox blood, but there's no doubt that it helps. With the right choice of swim, the ordinary groundbait will do all you need. If all the tench you can catch are there anyway, you won't catch a single extra one, for all the trouble and mess that ox blood involves.

That's tench fishing for June then; I can't wait to come to grips with the big gold 'uns and the little green 'uns, or didn't you know there are two sorts.

Part Four:
Baits

38 The maggot and the specimen hunter

A few weeks ago a reader asked why specimen-hunting anglers don't use maggots more.

The answer is simple; the maggot is not usually the best bait for catching specimen fish. It is too easily taken by unwanted small fish and even if you use a bunch of maggots, even small fish will suck out the insides, one by one. Nor will a bunch of maggots let you use as big a hook as you often need. Anything bigger than a size eight is difficult to bait up with maggots, however many you use.

Ones and twos

There's another thing—very often while you can get big fish eating maggots, you can't persuade them to take a bunch. They want them in ones or twos, but not in a bunch of more than two. I've known plenty of times when shy roach would take single maggot but not doubles.

Those are some of the reasons why I don't rank the maggot as my number one big-fish bait; but that doesn't mean I never use maggots or never catch big fish when I do use them. There are times when they can be useful.

For me, one of the advantages of maggots, perhaps the main advantage, is that by feeding enough into the water, you can persuade most kinds of fish to feed on them, even at times when those fish were feeding on some natural feed that was abundant in the water.

If the size of the big fish you're after, and the conditions in which you hope to hook it, let you use a fairly small hook and fine tackle with a fair chance of success, then maggots can often be used very effectively.

Knowing when and how to use maggots is important.

Last October, I caught a lot of barbel in the Kennet on maggots, using a bunch on a size 10 hook attached to 3lb bs line. I also lost three very large barbel because this tackle wasn't strong enough to stop them from going fast downstream beyond my power to follow because of bankside trees. If I'd hooked those fish on 9lb line and a size four hook, I'd have landed them; but you can't use maggots on that sort of tackle.

Maggots were not the bait to use for big barbel in that swim, though they gave me lots of sport with smaller barbel up to 7lb or so. But in some of the Hampshire Avon swims, I could have taken specimen barbel on maggots and fine tackle, because there the barbel have no reason to take off downstream and travel a couple of hundred yards.

Big roach, where you find them in a shoal that is unaccompanied by smaller fish, can often be persuaded to feed on maggots and I have had dozens of two-pounders so. Rudd behave similarly, but need less persuading to feed.

Good quantity

Generally speaking, though if you're going to succeed with maggots you need plenty. Half a gallon at least, for a day's fishing. If you haven't got that quantity I'd rather stick to some other bait. Here and there you can manage with less, especially in waters where you're likely to benefit by what other anglers throw in; but more often, you need a good quantity to get the fish really on to them, and to be able to keep chucking them in till the unwanted small fish have got a bellyful, so that bigger specimens get a chance to take your hook-bait. You can catch a record roach on a single maggot, if you've used a gallon to feed the small ones first!

I used to experiment, years, ago, with all kinds of different maggots, and with all sorts of colours. Only once in my whole life have I known the colour to make any difference; on that day I could get fish on yellow maggots but not on plain white ones.

Never have I found anything to beat ordinary maggots as bought from the tackle shop, for catching the better-class fish. Specials, pinkies, squats, you can keep the lot. I'm not going to argue that some of these may not help a contest angler to pick up a few more tiddlers; after all, he's liable to be fishing in noisy company in the worst hours of the day, in an indifferent swim, and the odd ounce may make all the difference. But for my kind of fishing, plain white maggots are all I need.

Some years ago, I left some dead eels in a bucket and later found that they'd fed the biggest, juiciest maggots I ever saw. They were as thick as an ordinary pencil and more than an inch long.

Not even chub

I used them as bait with high hopes, and not a fish would look at them. Not even chub. Perhaps I didn't give them a fair trial, if any reader wants to do it, all he needs is 10 or 12 lb of eels and plenty of fresh air all around!

Much more important than the kind of maggot is the way it is put on the hook, or I should perhaps say, the way the hook lets you put it on, for you want a hook with a small barb.

Here's a tip—if you have a bite on a maggot, and miss, change the maggot. Yes, even if it is unmarked. I don't say you will never get a bite on a maggot that has once been in a fish's mouth; I will say that your chances of a second bite, especially from a good fish, are reduced. You can't see anything wrong with that maggot, but often the fish can.

One thing I like about maggots; they sometimes tell you you've had a bite that you never saw. You wind up, and the maggot is just an empty skin. So you know at least one feeding roach, dace, or bream is about, and that you must watch for bites more carefully, if necessary changing to a more sensitive rig. *There have been plenty of winter days when a sucked-out maggot has told me fish were in my swim, and caused me to persevere and catch some, when I might otherwise have moved elsewhere.*

They're ideal

There's hardly a species of fish that won't take maggots, and they're ideal for the angler who fishes for 'anything that comes along'. But to hear anglers say it isn't worth going coarse fishing where maggots are barred, makes me want to spit. I suppose it shouldn't, though. All the more room for those who really know how to fish!

39 Lovely grub and all of it free!

Fred J Taylor has suggested that I tell you something about natural baits.

He and I have often arrived at the waterside without any bait, depending on what natural baits we could find, and we've usually managed to find something that caught us some fish. The first thing a baitless angler thinks of is digging for worms. At the waterside, it's usually a waste of time, all you get is two and a half miserable little brown worms and a centipede. You may, however find some nice red marshworms under a heap of weeds or rushes that have been left on the bank. They're fragile baits but the fish love 'em. You may also find some useful grubs by turning over dried cowpats. Fish like these too.

An old dead tree or fallen branch, with loose bark, may house a colony of woodlice or earwigs, both of which make excellent baits for roach and dace. If the timber is really rotten and full of holes, try knocking it to pieces, for it may hold grubs that will do well as bait. There are several beetles and moths whose larvae bore into rotten wood, and these larvae are appreciated by many sorts of fish.

Look for waterside plants and trees whose leaves have been eaten, because if you can find the caterpillars responsible, you can catch fish with them. There are dozens of different kinds, but the fish will eat all of them, from a little green smooth-skinned caterpillar to a great big 'woolly bear'.

Chub simply love beetles of all kinds, so do trout. Dace and rudd will eat any beetle small enough to go into their mouths; and they all like daddy-long-legs (craneflies) and grasshoppers. Grasshoppers take some catching, and even when caught, are apt to escape again; but it is often worth all the trouble because once on the hook, they're deadly baits.

If you see some rushes that look a bit yellow and seedy compared to their neighbours, pull them out and split the stems carefully, hoping to find a white grub inside. Izaak Walton knew all about these chaps, which are called flagworms. All kinds of fish go for them, as they also do for dock grubs, which are found by digging among the roots of dock plants. Here

150

again, you look for a seedy-looking dock and dig up its roots. Don't waste time digging healthy docks; leave those to flourish against the time you need a dock leaf for nettle stings.

You may find a wasp's nest, either buried or hanging on a tree. Whether you use its contents depends on your bravery and what facilities you have for taking it. The hanging sort isn't hard, cut it down so that it falls in a landing net, shove it straight under water, leave it there for a couple of hours, and then come back and cut it up. What fish won't take wasp grubs?

Various fruits, when in season can catch you fish, elderberries being perhaps the best known; but snowberries will catch chub and so will blackberries at times. You'd think hips and haws would catch fish, but I've never done any good with either. I caught a 3lb chub on a ripe sloe once.

Coming to baits that can be found actually in the water, I don't need to tell you that loach, minnows, and bullheads are all good baits for chub, trout, and perch. And you know all about caddis grubs, except perhaps that often they're better fished in their cases than pulled out. Three complete with cases on a No 6 hook make a fine bait for barbel and chub.

Water snails are eaten by many kinds of fish, but for some reason, they don't often succeed as hook-baits. I've caught tench, carp, and chub on water snails at times, and on land snails too, but more often than not these baits are ignored. Don't ask me why; but try snails, any sort, now and then. There's no telling when they may get you a good fish.

Enough has been written about mussels and crayfish in the last few years for every angler to know how and when to use these baits, but few take advantage of them, probably because they're scared to use really big baits. Don't be! Both crayfish and mussels can be deadly.

Like water-snails, freshwater shrimps are far from reliable. Sometimes they'll catch fish after fish; more often the fish won't touch them.

I once caught six roach in six casts on shrimps, and five of those roach were over 2lb. I thought I'd hit on a bait that would really catch the roach in that river. Since then, I've never had a bite when baiting with a freshwater shrimp. But try shrimps; like snails, they don't often succeed but when they do, the result can be very satisfactory.

Do you know what I mean by gravelly mud? If not, I don't

151

know how to explain it. It's a kind of gritty silt. In it you may find one or both of two creatures that are among the deadliest of all baits. One is the mayfly nymph, a creature ivory-buff in colour with six legs and three tail-whisks, and dark-brown rear segments. This will catch fish for sure. The other is the immature lamprey, which spends the first part of its life buried in this special kind of silt. It's blind at this stage and comes in all sizes from very tiny up to the size of a lobworm.

You have to scratch and rake in the mud to get these 'sand-grigs'; one way is to shovel the mud into a muslin or nylon net bag and then wash it in the river. I doubt if there is any more deadly bait for chub, trout, and barbel than a big 'sandgrig', or several small ones on a No 6 hook.

In lakes and ponds, you may find the rat-tailed maggot, which lives in the mud in very shallow water, and breathes by sticking a tube up to the surface. Watch for the tubes, not much thicker than hairs, coming out of the mud.

Under lily leaves and also on weeds, you can find little jelly sausages full of spots. Water-snail eggs, they are. Fish eat them! They also eat water-lily seeds at times.

Coming back to dry land, the larva of the cranefly, the leather-jacket, hated by all who cultivate grassland, is another very effective bait.

I could go on for pages; but there's a few 'naturals' to be going on with. Even when you've brought plenty of cheese, bread, or maggots, don't fail to try these natural baits now and then. You can often get fish with them that you wouldn't have caught otherwise.

40 Don't turn away from the worm

Not long ago I wrote about pastes. Now a lot of readers have asked for information about worms.

Nowadays, worms are neglected. There was a time when a worm of one kind or another was the favourite bait of most anglers. For coarse fish in Ireland, it still is. I don't hesitate to say that more good fish would be caught if more anglers used worms for bait, not always, but more often than they do now.

There are lots of different worms. There's the very common lobworm that grows to the size of an ordinary pencil. It comes to the surface on calm, mild, damp nights and lies there. This is the time to catch it, and the method of catching it has been described so well and so often that I don't need to repeat it now. It is a fallacy that lobworms need scouring before being used as bait. Keep them in damp moss, damp granulated peat, or damp newspaper, preferably with some pieces of damp rotten sacking mixed in. And keep them cool.

There is no species of fish that won't take lobworms, though some like them more than others. Those that are specially keen on them are perch, eels, trout, chub, barbel, bream, rudd, and tench. In some waters they are very good for carp. In flood water, roach take them well, so do dace. Many a pike, some big, have taken lobworms.

Good-sized hook

Fish them on good-sized hooks, usually size 6 or 8, or use their tails on a size 10.

The next most important worm in my book is the cockspur. This is rather like a miniature lobworm, but redder in colour. In my opinion it is far superior to the similar-sized brandling. The difference is that brandlings have alternate red and yellow bands round them, and give off a sort of yellowish fluid. The cockspur doesn't have the yellow bands and doesn't produce the fluid.

Anyone who has a garden, even a tiny one, can have a supply of cockspur worms. All you need is plenty of dead leaves and some soil. You build up alternate layers of leaves and soil, each an inch or so thick and if you leave it long enough, you'll find cockspur worms in it. It should be in a shaded place and you must keep it moist in dry weather.

If you can add bits of rotten sacking and some lawn mowings or rotten straw, you'll have more and bigger cockspur worms. But you mustn't overdo the lawn mowings or your heap will heat up and expel or kill the worms. You can add all sorts of vegetable matter, like tea leaves, apple peelings, cabbage leaves, and so on, but don't be too lavish because you must have a cool heap. Cockspurs like the heap kept in layers, so after digging it over to get your supply of the worms, restore the layers. A separate supply of dead leaves or partially rotted lawn mowings helps you to do this.

Depending on their size, you can fish cockspurs on hooks from size 14 to size 10. They'll catch most kinds of fish, specially in conditions when big lobworms don't seem to be very successful, but they're specially good for bream and rudd in almost any conditions you may find. Tench will often take them in clear water when they aren't too keen on lobs, and on some rivers, cockspurs are deadly for roach, grayling and dace in winter. Crucian carp are specially fond of cockspurs.

Lobworms failed

There are also times when big river perch will take a cockspur and refuse a big lobworm. I have seen Ken Taylor take fine bags of Ouse perch on cockspurs from swims in which he had tried lobworms in vain.

I suppose I shall have to talk about brandlings next. I've caught quite a lot of fish with them and I know many anglers who have plenty of confidence in them, but I haven't so much myself. I am sure they are inferior to cockspurs. You can get them from most tackle shops. They can also be found in unsavoury places into which such delightful substances as sewage and abattoir washings are discharged, as well as in rather wet, ancient manure heaps.

The next kind of worm I want to talk about is also a small one which lives in cultivated soil and also in muddy margins of lakes and rivers. It is about the size of a cockspur, but rather thicker in relation to its length, and olive green in colour. I don't know how to cultivate this sort of worm, but I can tell you that at times it is absolutely deadly for tench, fished on a size 10 hook. Other fish like rudd and bream take this small greenish worm but it is primarily a tench bait, though I've known it catch big crucian carp too.

If you fish tench lakes where the fish are specially shy and hard to catch, it is always well worth while to obtain a supply of green worms. They don't always succeed, no bait does, but I have known them catch tench when other baits like lobs, bread, cockspurs, maggots, and mussels had completely failed. As well as fishing them on the bottom, they can be tried at midwater.

Another worm that can be very useful at times is the marsh-worm or leen worm. You can find it sometimes under matted, rotting brown rushes at the waterside. It is about halfway in size, when fully grown, between a cockspur and a lobworm and is a fine iridescent red worm, with almost a greenish sheen on it.

Most kinds of fish like it, but the great drawback to it is that it is very fragile. It often breaks when being put on the hook and it won't stand up to anything more than very gentle casting. I find it useful for stret-pegging alongside the dead rushbeds in winter and have caught plenty of good roach, dace, and perch with it. Now and then, finding a colony of marshworms by accident in the summer has helped me catch good tench and bream. But the use of the worm is limited not only because it is scarce and fragile but because it is difficult to keep for any length of time.

Next on my list is the blue-headed worm. This is found in very fertile soil, the most likely source being in earth-floored chicken runs that have been in use for some considerable time. This is a big worm, as thick as a lob, longer, tougher, and light in colour, with a blue head and a light orange band. It is a very tough worm indeed and ideal for very long casting. Perch, tench, bream, and big rudd like it, to my certain knowledge and I don't doubt that other fish do, too.

Break up clods

Finally, there's the dry-soil pink worm. If you dig over culti-vated soil that is dry and compacted at the surface, you will find, if you break up the clods, that here and there is a round, closed hole in a clod that contains a long, thin, coral-pink worm rolled up in a ball.

I don't know a thing about the life history of these worms or how they live, but I do know that the hard work involved in col-lecting a few dozen isn't wasted because they're tough and deadly baits, specially for low, clear river conditions. They'll catch roach, dace, chub, and barbel in the gravelly runs be-tween streamer weeds, not to mention perch, trout, and gray-ling where these species are present. They'll also stay alive in temperatures that would quickly kill any other kind of worm.

Don't neglect worms. They can catch you plenty of big fish.

155

41 Carp baits

Nowadays there is much discussion among carp fishers about baits as there is among fly-fishers about fly patterns, and I sometimes wonder if the carp fishers have fallen into the age old error of seeking a magic bait that they expect to compensate for numerous short-comings in other aspects of carp fishing. It might therefore be a good idea to consider carp baits.

Carp will eat anything that is edible, if they've been educated to eat it and not educated to avoid it. That is the important thing to remember if you want to catch carp. It applies to most other fish, too, but to a lesser extent, and I'll explain why.

Any water can support a certain weight of fish, and it doesn't take long, after stocking a new water, for the fish, whatever kind they may be, to multiply and grow until this weight is reached. If the fish happen to be of species that grow to only modest sizes, such as roach, rudd, and perch, the water will hold very large numbers; but if the fish are of species that grow very large, then there will be far fewer of them.

The same supply of food that can produce 200 roach ranging from an ounce or two up to, say, 1lb, will only produce one 20lb carp. Consequently, any pond or lake will hold far fewer carp than it will fish of other species. This means that if much fishing goes on, a much greater percentage of the carp will soon become educated about what baits to avoid, because more of them will be hooked and lost, or caught and returned.

Carp also live much longer than such fish as roach, perch, rudd, etc, so there will be more old stagers who have had longer to learn. So you have to stay ahead of their education if you want to catch them consistently.

Protein nonsense

Lately, we've read and heard a lot about high protein baits for carp, and the notion has spread that your bait has got to be mighty meaty, matey, if you want carp to take it. Some people have gone further and used scientifically calculated high-protein baits made from synthetic ingredients.

It seems to me that this is a right load of nonsense. Carp are not expert dietitians, and even if they were, they're not equipped to carry out an analysis of a ball of paste lying on the bottom, to ascertain if its protein content is 39 per cent or 40 per cent. Nor do I believe that carp are particularly favourably inclined towards high protein, or meaty, baits. As I said earlier, they'll eat anything edible that they've been taught to eat.

If you owned a lake where no fishing ever took place, you could not only train the carp in it to eat practically any kind of food; you could even teach them to come and take it from your fingers. There are plenty of ornamental pools where that actually happens; and usually the favourite food is bread, which is very low indeed in protein. After a comparatively short time in its tank at the zoo aquarium, my record carp had learned to come to the top and take food from the hand of anyone who offered it; and it didn't care whether the food was bread or raw liver.

One of the most popular and effective baits of recent years is sweetcorn, and a fat lot of protein there is in that! The reason sweetcorn is so effective is that it has a pleasant flavour and, more important, consists of large numbers of particles that are all alike. I might add that when you hear a modern carp fisher talking about 'particle baits', ten to one what he means is sweetcorn.

You teach carp, and indeed other fish, very quickly when the same identical lesson is repeated over and over again, and that's what happens when you bait up with sweetcorn, or soaked sultanas, or anything else that consists of a lot of identical little bits of food. In fact, if you keep at it, you'll have the fish so preoccupied with it that they'll hardly look at anything else.

That's the way their small brains work, because that's the way most of their natural food comes, in a lot of little bits that are all alike, such as bloodworms, or daphnia.

Groundbait problems

But if, having trained the carp to eat whatever you've chosen for baiting-up, you proceed to use it as hook-bait and catch some of them, you'll very quickly teach them to avoid that bait, and you won't have to catch them all to do it, because one fish will follow the example of another. So eventually you'll have to abandon what was at first a successful bait and groundbait, and try something else.

On all waters, the business is complicated by the presence of natural food. If you're trying to teach carp to eat, say, sweetcorn, at the same time that a population explosion of daphnia is teaching them to eat those, you aren't likely to be very successful. And if, on heavily fished waters, one angler is trying to teach the carp to eat cat food, one is trying to teach them to eat boiled potato, and a third is pressing the attractions of sweetcorn on them, it is a matter of luck, quantity, and the preference of the fish, which of them beats the others, provided that some natural food doesn't keep the carp from eating any of them.

One more thing that may be important in big carp waters. There's a lot of evidence to show that carp associate their experience with the surroundings in which it happened. So a carp that has learned, by being caught, to avoid eating bread at one end of a large lake, may very likely have no fear of bread at the other end. Exactly how far this goes, we don't know, but carp fishers who fish big waters may find that a bait that has lost its usefulness in one place may still catch fish at some other spot.

Hook-bait samples

This we have learned about certain baits; that the best thing for baiting-up is samples of the hook-bait. In earlier days we used to bait-up with mashed, soaked bread and fish with paste, crust, flake, or paste and crust together. We'd have done better, I am sure, if we had made our groundbait up into a lot of identical balls.

It has to be remembered, throughout all this, that you don't catch carp just by getting your baiting-up and your hook-bait materials right. You have to choose the right spot, you have to choose the right tackle, you have to fish at the right time, and on well fished waters you'll do well to relate it all to what other anglers are doing. That's why I deplore the element of secrecy that seems to be creeping into carp fishing. It often results in anglers spoiling one anothers' chances, and in fewer fish being taken by everyone.

42 Stewed wheat

Lots of readers have written to ask me about stewed wheat—how to prepare it and how to use it.

There are many ways of stewing wheat, and opinions differ about how much it should be stewed. Fred Taylor, for example, likes his wheat grains well swollen, but showing only the slightest sign of splitting. I don't mind if the grains are well and truly split wide open, provided they are well swollen and nice and soft. We both like as big a grain as possible. This is decided partly by how big the grains are as bought, and partly by the way in which they're cooked. I buy the best wheat I can, it's cheap enough!

The well known thermos flask method of stewing wheat is convenient and reasonably satisfactory, but definitely not as good as pre-soaking and careful stewing.

To make the best of wheat, soak it in cold water for at least twenty-four hours; then bring it to the boil, turn down the heat and stew as slowly as you possibly can. Or you can bring it to the boil, let it cool, bring to the boil again, and so on, till the grains have reached the stage you prefer. I am sure that extra trouble taken in stewing your wheat is well worth while. A big plump grain whose husk is firm yet soft enough not to impede hook penetration is what you want.

Cook it slowly

Such a well prepared grain allows you to stick your hook through the husk, whereas a grain that has been cooked too fast will be split, but will have a hard, horny husk from which the hook won't come easily on the strike. That means worse than missed fish, it means fish which you feel briefly, then they're off. A fish missed clean may come again; a pricked or scratched one usually bolts and may take other fish with it.

In waters holding many minnows, wheat will often get you splendid roach, dace, or bream where because of the minnows, maggots, crust, paste, or small worms are nearly useless. I fish it on a No 12 round-bend gilt hook as a rule, but where fish are extra big and stronger tackle is advisable. I often use two grains on a No 10. With that, a soft husk is of paramount importance.

Many anglers advise against sticking the hook through the husk at all, but provided your wheat is properly prepared, you'll find penetrating the husk keeps the grain on the hook much better and still allows the hook to be struck home. I make an exception in the case of the roach pole, however, which lets you put a bait into the water so gently that there is no need for the hook to penetrate the husk. You can just nick it into the exposed white part of the grain.

Wheat can be fished on ordinary tackle by all the well known methods; there are no special techniques necessary for using it, nor are the bites obtained any different from those you get with paste or maggots. What you have to watch is not so much your tackle choice and manipulation, but the matter of groundbaiting.

Wheat is very solid stuff indeed. That means that its rate of sinking is much higher than that of maggots or bread-based groundbaits. In running water it will reach the bottom much nearer the place where it was thrown in, and an angler used to other baits and groundbaits can ruin his chances if he forgets this. He'll be fishing too far downstream from his groundbait.

Fills fish up

Not only does wheat sink fast, it fills fish up quickly. Over-groundbaiting is all too easy, especially with roach and dace. For any given swim, a quarter as much wheat as you'd use of maggots will be about right.

Also, because of its weight, wheat isn't the best bait to choose to fish over a bottom made of thin mud or silkweed. Too much sinks in. Use it mainly for clean gravel-bottomed swims, or clean clay.

Wheat is a good bait at any time of the season, but specially so for the six or seven weeks immediately following harvest-time. If you haven't used it before, give it a trial—but make sure you prepare it properly.

43 Bread flake

Lately, I have had several letters from readers asking for advice on the use of flake as bait. Before giving any, I have to explain that there are two kinds of flake.

One is an old favourite of Thames and Lea anglers and is sometimes called 'golden flake'. It consists of the layer of golden crust that lies between the top crust of a loaf, and the crumb. Preparing it takes time.

Roach pole bait

You soak the loaf, then, with a sharp knife, pare off the top layer of well baked outer crust. Then slice off the layer underneath, without cutting into the white. This is your golden flake. It must come from a part of the loaf that hasn't touched the tin in which the loaf was baked. The part that has touched the tin is what you mash up for groundbait, without much white mixed up with it. Pieces of the golden flake are torn off for hook-bait, and the old experts used to insist on a No 9 gilt crystal hook for fishing it.

It doesn't stay on the hook at all well, and it wouldn't be entirely wrong to describe it as a roach pole bait, for with the pole you can lower it into the swim, and lift it out carefully when necessary. The roach pole isn't everyone's choice of weapon, and it certainly isn't quite as wonderful a weapon as many of its advocates would have us believe. One of its great advantages, however, is its ability to fish a soft fragile bait, like golden flake, without difficulty provided the fish you're after are within its reach, and not of a species and size beyond its ability to cope with if you hook them.

The other kind of flake is the better known one, consisting of a pinch of the white crumb of a new loaf. This is a very good bait for many kinds of fish, but it is decidedly tricky to use.

The whole secret

The whole secret of using it successfully is in knowing how to put it on the hook, and that applies whether you're using a tiny speck on a No 20 or a great lump on the No 2. If you squeeze new bread too hard, you get a solid piece that won't soften in the water for a long while, and which can all too easily get in the way of the hook point when a fish takes and you strike. But if you don't pinch your bit of flake firmly enough on to the hook, it won't sink properly when you want it to, and it comes off the hook at the least provocation. There are several ways of avoiding these troubles, but it does take a little experience to get every bait right.

When you pull off a bit of new bread crumb, you'll find that some of it tears away in the form of a flat layer. If you lay a bit of this on your hook shank and fold it over, away from the point, you will find that pinching it against the shank holds it pretty well, yet leaves some nice feathery edges to attract fish. Whether the bait tends to sink or float depends upon how big you make the pinched part in relation to the part left unpinched, and only practice will teach you to get it right. Whatever you do, don't get any of it pinched over the bend, point and barb of the hook.

The fish won't mind if a bit of hook shows, but if you don't believe me about that, paint the hook white, but whatever you do, don't blob pinched flake over that hook point, for it will spoil your chances of fish.

Remember that new bread flake swells up considerably in the water, so let your bait be about half the size you want it to reach eventually. At the same time, you needn't be afraid of fishing a fair-sized bit of flake, because after it has swollen, which it does very quickly, it becomes very soft, except where it has been pinched, and fish find it easy to suck in.

The new loaf from which you get your flake cannot easily be used as well to make groundbait, for if you try to soak and mash it up, you'll get a horrid sticky mess that can't be thrown accurately and the sinking rate of which is quite unpredictable.

Don't do that

So for groundbait, use a loaf a day or more old. That makes a nice groundbait. All it needs is a good soaking in cold water, followed by a squeezing out of surplus water and thorough mashing-up.

Don't go and mix a lot of bran or toppings with it, to produce

162

a brown unappetizing set of lumps. If it has to be dried off, use bread crumbs, which you can either buy ready for use or make yourself by mincing up slices of bread that you've got bone dry. Or you can use sausage rusk, but that can make your groundbait sink too slowly for quick water.

There's nothing special about the methods of using newbread flake. You fish it in ordinary simple ways. It's a good bait, but not so good as to compensate for bad fishing. No bait is quite that good.

44 Why fish like hemp

Hempseed is a bait still misunderstood by many anglers. For example I noticed that in a recent *Angling Times* a reader asked why only roach eat the seed bait.

Well, other fish eat hempseed too. It's a good bait for dace, and until, for some totally inexplicable reason it was barred, it caught lots of barbel from the Throop fishery on the Stour. I've caught chub on it from time to time and once or twice I've baited up tench pitches with it and had fair catches.

A grain of stewed hemp looks astonishingly like a tiny freshwater mussel, and it has been suggested many times that that's what fish take it for. That may be right, but I think what fish take a grain of hemp for is a grain of hemp, like they take a grain of stewed wheat for a grain of stewed wheat, or a grain of sweetcorn for a grain of sweetcorn. They don't need to see any resemblance between these grains and anything else.

Hemp is very nutritious food. In experiments carried out between the wars, roach and dace were found to grow quickly and stay very healthy when fed on hempseed. Yet we still hear the old nonsense about hemp doping fish. Not long ago, a senior police officer being interviewed on TV said hempseed was a dope, but the police didn't mind anglers using it for bait, because only fish would be hooked on it, ha, ha, ha.

So let's get it straight. There is no hashish, or 'grass' or any other dope, in hempseed. If you plant the seed, which is illegal, you can grow a plant from it that can be used to make hashish. Boiled hemp, however, can't grow so if you spill some on the river bank, you aren't likely to arrive there months later to find a hippy community in possession.

Complaint

The fact that boiled hemp can't grow also answers the complaint that it grows on the bottom and chokes the water with weed. Yes, that complaint has been made, in all seriousness! Is there any real and justified objection to the use of hempseed as bait and groundbait? In my opinion, there is not. But what can cause trouble is the misuse of hempseed.

Fish tend to feed selectively on whatever food is available in the greatest quantity. If the food consists of great numbers of very small bits, all alike, then fish become preoccupied, refusing all other kinds of food. Hempseed happens to be about the most preoccupying bait we know. If large numbers of anglers keep on throwing large quantities of hemp into a water, it doesn't take long for the fish to reach a state when they won't look at anything else. At the same time, the fish very quickly become full-fed and then they stop feeding altogether for a time.

This is why some anglers object to hemp. If it is misused, it first produces a situation where it is the only successful bait. Then it moves on to the stage when the catches, even on hemp, start getting smaller and smaller. Human nature being what it is, and in spite of words of wisdom we get from brilliant anglers like Ivan Marks, the average angler's response to a falling-off in his catching rate is to heave in more groundbait. In the case of hemp, this falling-off is usually due to the fish being stuffed to the back teeth with hemp. So the extra quantity thrown in will keep them that way, not only for hours but, in some cases, for days. What they can't eat right away lies on the bottom and is picked up next day, and the day after.

Favourite

I've seen this sort of thing happening, on more than one water. There used to be a favourite spot of mine where I caught roach, good roach, with a two-pounder now and then. This water was at that time open to anyone to fish, free of charge, and you can bet that a lot of people did fish it. The result was that fishing on a Monday or Tuesday was a complete waste of time. The Sunday hemp bombardment saw to that.

Early on Wednesday morning, you could make a nice catch of roach on crust or stewed wheat. Wednesday afternoon was early closing day at the nearby town, so the hemp hail recommenced at about 2 pm. It wasn't as heavy as the Sunday one, so you could start catching roach again by Thursday evening and Friday was the best day.

Saturday morning was good, but on Saturday afternoon the hemp was going in again, its quantity varying according to various sporting activities in the region, such as the Test match at the Oval or the Spurs playing at home.

Sunday, of course, saw the resumption of carpet bombing, from anglers sitting at 10yd intervals. They caught relatively little, and the fish they caught were mainly small. Their usual practice was to flick in a dozen grains, then cast among the sinking grains with tackle set to fish about 2 to 3ft deep in a 7 to 8ft swim.

Undersized roach intercepted the hemp as it sank, as well as the shot of such anglers who hadn't got around to using lead wire instead. There were lightning dives, twitches, lifts, and trembles of the floats, at which the anglers would strike as fast as possible, sometimes hooking a little roach—somewhere. Not infrequently, a pathetic little top lip was found on the hook.

Hemp was naturally blamed for this state of affairs, especially by the more experienced anglers, and not entirely without reason. But the truth was that it was the majority of anglers, not the hempseed, that was to blame. The same thing would have happened if the bait had been pearl barley, or wheat, hurled in in the same quantities and having the same fish-filling effect. You can even do it with maggots, or casters, but they're not as filling as hemp or other seed baits, and nowadays the cost would probably prevent over-feeding to a large extent.

In the days I'm talking about, hemp was so cheap that everyone, even the kids, could afford a quart or so.

The remedy for excessive groundbaiting is simple. Don't do it! If every angler realized that if you use more groundbait than is necessary, whatever it may be, you're spoiling your own sport, we'd all do better—and save money as well.

Half pint

Half a pint of hempseed is enough for a day's fishing anywhere. By using it sparingly, you don't get lots of small fish going mad at all depths. You keep the fish feeding at the bottom, and you catch the bigger specimens. If you do find your bait being intercepted at half-depth, use a bait dropper, or enclose a good pinch of seed in a ball of cereal groundbait. If you want the quality fish, keep your hook dragging bottom, or, in still waters, use a small float fished on lift tackle.

I like to fish two or three grains on a No 10 or No 12 hook. That also helps you to avoid the small fish, and if you're after barbel, it lets you use a stronger line. Don't forget to let the hook point show, whether you use one grain or several. If you need to fish at a distance, use an open-ended swimfeeder, fill it with hemp and dry cereal, and block it with damp groundbait. That'll empty itself right where your baited hook is.

Hempseed can be an excellent bait used correctly, but there's nothing to beat it for spoiling sport if it is used wrongly.

Part Five:
Tackle

45 Four leads I use for all my fishing

Lately, quite a number of readers have been writing to ask me about the different kinds of lead they see on sale in the shops. There are many sorts, which must be confusing to the novice.

I only use three sorts, or four, if you count split-shot. For spinning, I use Wye leads. There are others that may work equally well, but I'd rather have the Wye ones. For live-baiting, which I do very rarely and only when I know the whereabouts of a pike and have first tried him with a deadbait, I prefer barleycorn leads. For legering and paternostering—two methods which are due to the development of what some call a link leger and others a running paternoster—I use either Arlesey bombs or swan-shot.

I use wire

If I am float-fishing, of course I use split shot like everyone else, but if I did any hempseed fishing, I'd use lead wire instead. Perhaps I should explain that I'm not against hempseed; it's just that where I fish, I've got no reason to use it. That's the lot. I don't use coffin leads, spiral leads, geen leads, pierced bullets, or any of the fancy anti-kink leads that have been invented at various times.

The reason I prefer the Wye lead when I spin is, that I've always found it reliable. It prevents line-twist due to the action of the spinner quite successfully, and has less tendency to catch on snags than other leads.

The Arlesey bomb

Wye lead

Two knots

Having the right lead, as far as weight is concerned, is as important in spinning as in legering, and some anglers consider the Wye lead too much trouble to change. This can be avoided if the trace is of nylon, because changing leads involves only two half-blood knots which are very easy to tie.* In the case of wire traces, the angler who makes his own from single strand alasticum wire can incorporate link-swivels at the trace ends, one for attaching the bait and the other for attaching the lead.

All you need for live baiting, of course, is a barleycorn lead slid on the line after attaching the float but before attaching the trace.

When it comes to what, sooner or later, we shall have to call legernostering the choice of lead depends on the circumstances. When really long casting is needed there's still nothing to equal the Arlesey bomb. Its streamlined shape minimizes wind resistance and its swivel reduces almost to nil the chance of the tackle twisting or tangling in flight. It also makes a good general-purpose lead; but nowadays, especially for river fishing, I use the swan-shot leger most of the time.

Simple rig

I've come to the conclusion that this simple rig is one of the greatest benefits to the leger angler that was ever invented. Fred J Taylor ought to get an OBE for thinking out the basic principle, and I should get at least a tiny cheer for simplifying it to the stage where all an angler needs to go legering is a box of swan-

* I now use the Grinner knot

shot, in addition to his normal equipment. It's the best leger I know of, for fast water, weedy water, or snaggy water, or any combination of those three. The only conditions in which the Arlesey bomb decidedly beats it is when a very long throw is needed.

Some readers will be wondering by now why I haven't mentioned various flat leads, which are supposed to hold bottom in fast water. Well, I'm not at all convinced that flat leads do hold bottom very well, always supposing I want a lead to hold, which I seldom do. I reckon that a string of swan-shot will hold better than the same weight of lead in any other form. Try it yourself. Choose a really fast run and see which holds best, a string of sixteen swan-shot or an ounce coffin lead.

Shot are lost

Test also which is easier to control when you want to move the lead a bit. Consider also which is cheaper to lose, bearing in mind that losing the coffin lead means losing the hook too, whereas only the swan-shot are lost when they get caught in a snag. Of course when it comes to regulating your weight of lead to fine limits, the swan-shot leger has all other types well beaten. In fact the accuracy with which your weight can be regulated is one of the swan-shot leger's main advantages.

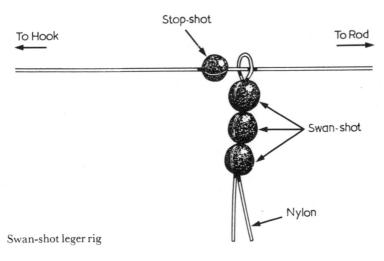

Swan-shot leger rig

171

The principles of the swan-shot leger can be used for still-water fishing by adding a few small bored corks to the string of shot. These, chosen correctly can result in a leger weighing half an ounce or more in the air but next to nothing in the water, allowing longer casting, reducing the tendency of the weight to sink into a soft bottom, but still allowing a fish to draw line if the leger is caught up. One useful tip about swan-shot legers: make the nylon loop out of your running line, or from a stronger line, not a thinner or weaker one. That way it will slide easier. If the leads are caught up, they'll slide off the loop.

In very weedy water, or for fishing a silkweed covered bottom, you can use a long string of smaller shot instead of the swan-shot. And if you think you may want to change to float legering or even long-trotting, just put two rubber tube float caps on the running line before making up your leger. Then you can easily add whatever float you fancy, or remove it. You can adjust your shot to suit the float by pulling some off your nylon loop, or pinching more on.

To the angler who is roving from swim to swim, which often pays, especially when seeking perch or chub, this easily changed rig is of considerable benefit. A few weeks ago, having searched a big open swim with a light leger, I decided to try trotting a big pelican quill float down, beyond the distance to which the leger could be cast. All I had to do was attach that float by the rubber caps already on the line and remove one-swan shot.

Eleven chub

I was glad I tried it, for I got nine chub up to 4½lb, and a 3¼lb perch. All I'd caught on the leger was a dace of about 4oz.

The very next day, in another swim, I couldn't touch a fish on the float tackle; so I unshipped the float, added two more shot on the nylon loop, and in the next two hours I got eleven chub up to 3½lb from a hole in the river bed that the float tackle couldn't reach.

Those of you who haven't tried the swan-shot leger are definitely missing something good.

172

46 Think about the water before you choose a fly rod

At this time of year I always receive lots of letters asking for advice about fly-fishing, mostly trout fishing. Some readers want to know which rods, reels, lines, leaders, and flies they should buy, others want information about casting. Let's take the tackle question first.

Trout fishing varies enormously, from tiny brooks to big rivers and reservoirs, and what might be suitable for one kind of water would be quite wrong for another. So before choosing a fly rod it is essential that you know what kind of water you intend to fish.

A small brook would probably be best suited by a little rod of from 7ft to 8ft in length, carrying a No 5 line. Classic chalk streams like the Test or Itchen might need a rod of 8ft to 9ft, using a No 6 or No 7 line. Larger, rain-fed rivers where most of the fishing would be done with wet flies might need a flexible rod of 8ft to 10ft but carrying a lighter line, No 5 perhaps, and such an outfit would also do very well for boat fishing on a loch or reservoir. For fishing from the bank on larger lakes and reservoirs, a rod of 9ft to 9½ft capable of casting a No 8 or No 9 line would be a good choice.

In the case of rods from 7ft to 8½ft, taking lines up to No 5 or No 6, and where accuracy is of greater importance than distance, I prefer split-cane rods, although this is a personal preference, as there are some nice hollow glass rods in this range.

For long rods, and long casting, I like glass rods best, mainly because it is possible to make them very much lighter than split-cane ones of similar length and power. This is particularly true of reservoir rods. I have a cane rod 9ft 3in in length, taking a No 8 line, which weighs 6½oz. I don't use it nowadays because my hollow glass reservoir rod of the same length and taking the same line weighs only 3¾oz. That makes it possible to go on casting much longer without getting tired, and the glass rod will outcast the cane rod by about 10yd.*

* Carbon fibre rods have now superseded both cane and fibreglass

Nonsense

A fly reel cannot be too light. Don't believe anyone who tells you that the reel must balance the rod. It's nonsense. All fly rods cast best with no reel on them at all. Therefore use the lightest reel that will carry all the line and backing you need; that will recover line reasonably quickly, and which has an exposed flange or rim to allow finger control. Single-action reels (non-geared) should be around 3½in in diameter for waters where there are big trout that may run a long way when hooked. For brook work, a very small reel, 2¾in to 3in in diameter, is fine.

If you choose a multiplier, get a lightweight one. I don't like too high a gear ratio, and about 1¾ to 1 seems to me ideal. For brooks and small rivers you don't need a lot of line; 12yd of fly-line and 50yd of backing is plenty. On big lakes and reservoirs, you need twice as much backing, at least, so that means a bigger reel.

There is an immense range of fly-lines available, which must confuse beginners horribly. There are level lines, double tapers, forward tapers, made of all sorts of different materials; some float, some sink slowly, some sink fast, some have sinking tips, and so on.

For a beginner intending to fish smallish rivers. I'd advise buying half a double-taper plastic floater, and needle-knotting it to monofil backing, about 20lb to 25lb bs. The size will of course be chosen to suit the rod; if in doubt about the exact size, choose a slightly heavier rather than a lighter line.

For lake and reservoir fishing from the bank, you'll need a floater and a sinker, and if you intend learning long casting, you'd better make your fly-lines 10yd long. Again, the size is chosen to suit the rod. You can use the same kind of backing, but more of it. I wouldn't advise choosing a very fast-sinking line at first; let your two lines be a floater and a slow sinker. When you've learned to cast pretty well you can add a fast sinker to your armoury.

In my opinion, there is no advantage in using a full 30yd line in any kind of trout fly-fishing that I've ever done or seen. It takes a very good caster to aerialize half that length. Nobody can drop a fly delicately and accurately at a distance greater than about 20yd. The tournament accuracy event uses 30in hoops, the farthest being 13⅓yd from the casting platform!

174

If you have a 15yd fly-line for river fishing, with a 3yd leader, you can put down your fly at 18yd and still have fly-line in your left hand. If you want more distance, you can shoot some backing. In more than forty years of fishing, I have never had to cast as much as 18yd to catch a river trout.

In reservoir fishing from the bank, a 10yd fly-line is a comfortable amount for a beginner to aerialize and when a very long throw is required, it is obtained by shooting a lot of nylon backing. You can cast well over 40yd with a 10yd fly-line. When you've become proficient, you may decide to use 12 or 13yd of floater, instead of only ten, for accurate covering of surface-feeding trout that rise within the limits of accurate and delicate fishing, which is up to about 17 or 18yd, if you're really good!

Distance

Apart from such conditions, and especially when you're using the sinking line, you're simply covering water and no great accuracy or delicacy are needed. You can then aerialize all your fly-line and get your distance by shooting lots of backing.

Now about casting. If you can afford professional coaching, do! If not, here are a few pointers. No matter what anyone else may tell you, stand with your left foot forward, if you're a right-handed caster. Use a stance similar to what you'd adopt to shoot with a longbow, or serve at tennis. This is important because it allows you to turn your head and watch your back-cast. You can see if you get your back-cast wrong and correct the fault. It's essential to do that because unless you make a good back-cast, you can't make a good forward-cast. When you've become proficient, you can put your feet anyhow you like; you can cast sitting, kneeling or even lying down, but while you're learning, let it be left foot forward.

Next thing is to remember that fly-casting differs from bait-casting, and also from tennis, golf, cricket, or any other game, in that the backwards movement needs power. In anything else, you can take the rod, the racket, the club, or the bat back quite slowly. Not in fly-casting! It needs some force, not great, to send the line back behind you and to set it up, so to speak, ready for the forward stroke. Unfortunately your arm and shoulder aren't very well designed for throwing the line backwards, which is why you need to give the back-cast special attention.

Any monkey can perform a good forward-casting action, but it's only when that follows a good back-cast that you can produce a good forward-cast. That's why it's so important, at first, to stand so that you can see your own back-cast.

47 Lines

In a recent issue of *Angling Times*, Ivan Marks gave a lot of helpful advice about monofil, which I would like to supplement this week. But first, a small difference of opinion!

Despite what Ivan said, there *has* been quite a useful improvement in nylon over the last twenty years. When first introduced, nylon ten thou' thick had a dry breaking strain of between 4 and 5lb. Now, even in the cheaper kinds, nylon of the same thickness has a dry breaking strain of about 7lb.

That's a greater improvement than you might think, because if you choose your line on breaking strain instead of thickness, it means a line 8 thou' thick nowadays is as strong as one 10 thou' thick, twenty years ago. And the stiffness of a line varies with the fourth power of the thickness; so 8 thou' line is nearly 60 per cent more flexible than 10 thou' line. In other words, we've not only had a useful improvement in strength, but a far greater improvement in flexibility.

And as Ivan rightly remarks, 'a supple, as opposed to a stiff hook-length gives you far more bites'. This is partly because the bait moves more naturally with currents, or falls more naturally when sinking in stillwater, and partly because the more supple the nylon is, the less the fish feel it when they take the bait.

Light

Ivan is also right about the effect of ultra-violet light on nylon. Every time you go fishing in daylight, your line is weakened, and the brighter the light, the more weakening there is. This effect is minimized by dyeing the line in any of the shades from yellow through buff, light brown and dark brown, to black.

There is another weakening effect caused by what is known as wet oxidation. Both wetness and temperature are involved in this. If you put away your reel, carrying wet nylon line, in a warm place, where the air can't get at it to let it dry, your line can lose a lot of strength. I've known nylon lose three-quarters of its strength between one weekend and another. Used through a couple of sunny days, it got a good dose of ultra-violet. Then it was left in a tackle box, in the boot of a car that stood in the sun all day for the next five days. Warm but damp, you see.

What is also important to realize is that the thinner the line is, the greater is the weakening effect. Take two lines, one 5 thou' thick and the other 10 thou' thick, and assume that the combined effects of ultra-violet and wet oxidation penetrate to a depth of a thousandth of an inch from the outer surface of the line. Your 5 thou' line will then be only 3 thou' thick, effectively. It will have lost nearly two-thirds of its strength. The 10 thou' line will be effectively 8 thou' thick and will have lost only about one-third of its strength. So the finer the line you use, the more careful you have to be about testing it between every outing, and doing your best to minimize the causes of weakening.

One way of doing so is by soaking the line in a 10 per cent solution of silver nitrate for 24 hours, then transferring the line to a photographic developer. That turns the line a deep chestnut colour, which not only keeps out the ultra-violet light but also protects against wet oxidation. Silver nitrate solution is expensive, and will stain your skin deep black, and nothing will shift it; you have to let it wear off. But you'll be amazed how long a silver nitrate treated monofil line will last.

There are lots of fallacies about nylon. One is that the thinner the line is, the easier it is to control in a wind. In fact the opposite is true. The reason is that although the air resistance decreases with the line thickness, the weight decreases in an even higher proportion. Halve the thickness and you reduce the weight by a quarter. So you'll have half the weight for any given wind pressure, and the line will blow about twice as much. So use as a heavy line as will give you the casting distance you need, if you're fishing on a windy day, unless, of course, you're legering in a strong current, and are concerned about water pressure on the line. Using a heavy running line doesn't mean you've got to put up with fewer bites, because you can always use a finer hook length.

Another point to watch with nylon lines is the effect of sliding a float, with one or more rubbers, up or down the line when it is dry. This can generate enough heat to weaken the line considerably. The heat is built up underneath the rubber and the damage is done not while you're moving the float along the line, but when you stop. All the heat that has built up under the rubber is then applied to one place in the line. You can't tell it has happened, so you cast out, get a bite, strike, and 'Oh dear, my line's parted at the float, however did that happen? Must have been a weak spot.' Yes, there was a weak spot, and you produced it!

The matter of pre-stretched line isn't quite as simple as is generally supposed. If any material is stretched within what is known as its elastic limit, and then released, its strength is not affected. But if it is stretched beyond its elastic limit, but short of breakage, and released, then when a load is next applied, the breaking strain will be found to have increased.

The reason is that the chains of molecules of which the material is made are lying more or less at random in the unstretched line, but after stretching beyond the elastic limit, these molecule chains are pulled into an approximately parallel position. They're all taking the load in unison, so the line is actually stronger against a steady load. Unfortunately, it won't stand up to a sudden jerk as well.

Easy clutch

Personally, I go along with Ivan Marks and seldom use pre-stretched lines, but I wouldn't discount their value in some sorts of fishing. You can get elasticity from your rod as well as from your line.

The trouble is that most match anglers use lines that are too weak in relation to the test-curve of their rods. Few rods have test-curves of less than half a pound, which means using lines no weaker than $1\frac{3}{4}$lb breaking strain. Allowing a reduction in strength of about 40 per cent by knotting and soaking, that means a dry breaking strain of around 3lb—and that is for a new line in perfect condition. Using anything finer is pushing your luck a bit, specially if your line is pre-stretched. With normal, unstretched nylon, the stretch compensates for what, as I calculate, are over-stiff match rods.

178

48 The science of hook design

I'm always getting queries about hook shapes and I often read articles and letters strongly advocating various types of hook. So this week I'm going to try to explain the factors that determine how a hook behaves.

Have a look at the diagrams (on page 00). You'll see a common sort of hook with what looks like two lines coming away from the end of the shank E. Actually, one of those lines is in the position it will take up when the point of the hook is just starting to penetrate. The other is in the position it takes up when the hook has gone as far as it can.

It may surprise a lot of anglers to find that from the instant the hook starts to penetrate, until it is fully home, the line is never a continuation of the shank. There is always an angle between the shank and the nylon.

Some of you match fishers might ponder about whether it is really a good idea to have your nylon whipped to the inside of the hook-shank, where it will twang back and forth across the end of the shank when you have a good fish on; or whether it wouldn't be better to whip the nylon to the back of the shank, as I have done for the last twenty years for all whipped-on hooks.

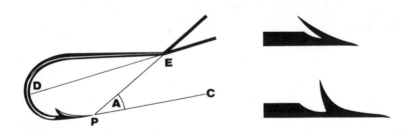

Hook design: (*left*) if the length of the shank DE is decreased, the angle of penetration (A) increases; (*above right*) correct design with the barb small and near the point; (*below right*) incorrect design with a deeply cut barb too far from the point and at a steep angle

Shank lengths

Now let's consider angle of penetration. This is the angle formed by the two lines EP and PC in the diagram. I've labelled it A. (Don't run away, I'm not going to blind you with science!)

Look at the diagram and you'll see that if the length of the shank is decreased without altering the hook in any other way, the angle of penetration will get bigger. It will take more force to stick the hook in if this angle gets bigger. If we reduce the shank so much that it is directly opposite the point, that point will have no tendency to penetrate at all.

With a round-bend hook, the depth to which it will penetrate will be determined by the point on the bend furthest from the end of the shank. That is, of course, looking at matters from the point of view of how much of the hook is buried. It won't make much difference to that even if we alter the length of the shank quite a lot, provided we don't shorten it so much that the hook won't penetrate at all.

Weak point

But alterations in shank length will affect how far below the surface of what is being penetrated the point will go. It'll go further with a shorter-shanked hook than with a longer-shanked hook, within reasonable limits, but as we found earlier, it takes more force to make a short shank-hook go home than it does with a longer-shanked hook.

Now what about the argument on outpoint *v* incurved hooks?

Look at the diagram again and visualize the hook point being angled outwards more. The angle of penetration A will increase. The effect will be the same as if we had shortened the shank. The hook will penetrate deeper and more force will be needed to make it do so. Now imagine the point curved inwards instead of outwards. This has the same effect as lengthening the shank. The hook won't penetrate so deeply below the surface of what it is penetrating, but it'll pull in as far as it can go a lot more easily. But curve it in too far and it won't penetrate at all.

One more thing. Although an incurved hook won't penetrate so deeply, the leverage that tends to break off or open out the points will be less than with an outpoint hook. Leverage can be important. You can see where it is likeliest to cause bending or breakage at D. So there is good reason for using a tapered design in which the thickness of wire at A is greater than at any other place. That way you get a stronger hook for a given weight of metal.

Now let's consider barbs and points.

Everything points to the advantage of a small barb. It doesn't require a big barb to prevent a hook from falling out. Barbs are not stuck on. They're cut from the wire from which the hook is made. The bigger the barb, the deeper the wire must be cut to make it and the weaker the hook becomes. And the more force you need to get the hook in past the barb. So you will see that a short-shanked outpoint hook with a deeply-cut barb, has three factors requiring extra force to make it penetrate and a weak place where all this extra force can cause breakage, behind the barb. To make matters even worse, we could cut the barb a long way back from the point, putting it nearer the place where maximum leverage is applied and still further increasing the force needed to drive it fully home.

Faulty barbs

We can add the final touch by cocking the barb up at a steep angle so it's even harder to get the hook properly home. I've drawn a couple of sketches of hook-points and barbs and I don't have to tell you which is good and which is bad. The bad one is exaggerated, of course, to show you what the tendencies are.

I have never yet seen a commercially made hook in which the barb wasn't too big, too deeply cut, too far from the point and cocked up too much. Some hooks are much better than others but all have these failings at least to some extent. John Bickerdyke pointed this out in the last century. Since then, hookmakers have not only disregarded his wise and sound comments, but actually seem in general, to have cut barbs deeper and raised them higher than they used ever to do in the nineteenth century.

What about shape?

Any sharp change of direction in the run of the hook wire is a weak place and for that reason I prefer round-bend to square-bend hooks, or to crystal hooks which are so popular. There seems to be a small advantage in having the point slightly snecked or reversed, ie fractionally out of the same plane as the rest of the hook, but it only needs a few degrees, five at most, otherwise the angle of penetration is increased too much.

Now we've seen, haven't we, that whether you shorten or lengthen the shank, you lose on the swings what you gain on the roundabouts, so to speak? What's the best compromise? Well, I'd say that in a general purpose hook, the distance ED in the diagram ought to be about two and a half times the gape. I think we should stick to that except where we have very special reasons to do otherwise. For example, you need a longer shank if you're tying floating limitations of mayflies. I like a somewhat shorter shank for fishing stewed wheat. But don't go to extremes either way.

Part Six:

What Lies Ahead?

49 What lies ahead?

I don't own a crystal ball, and have no faith whatever in astrology. I am therefore poorly qualified to predict what the future may hold for the sport of angling. All I can do is draw attention, both to the evils that afflict the sport and the measures that can and may be taken to counteract these evils.

Let me say at once that the angler is his own worst enemy, in more ways than one. He leaves huge quantities of litter at the waterside, which includes discarded line that entangles birds, causing them suffering and death. His discarded plastic bags, tins, and broken bottles injure and sometimes kill farm animals. Not uncommonly he leaves gates open, allowing these animals to stray. Specially if he is a sea angler, he treats his capture cruelly, often before the eyes of large numbers of non-anglers. Not all behave so; too many do.

While the angler is extravagant in his purchase of tackle and bait, he is parsimonious in the extreme in supporting his own organizations that strive to prevent damage to his fishing facilities. Out of three million anglers, only 20,000 join the Anglers' Co-operative Association, which fights pollution of waters to an extent solely determined by its finances. He turns down a proposal to increase subscriptions to the National Federation of Anglers by 3p per year. He resists by every possible means any increase in rod licence fees, which provide finance for the fisheries departments of the regional water authorities. Yet the sum required from him by these three bodies does not amount to half the cost of one single day's fishing.

Angling waters are affected directly by pollution, mainly poorly treated domestic sewage, but also industrial effluents, farm chemicals in a huge variety, fertilizers and, increasingly, the effluent from trout farms. In increasing its weight by 1lb, a trout excretes about 13oz. A trout farm that rears 30,000 trout puts 10 tons of trout excreta into the river from which it draws its water and returns it. Every kind of pollution is increased in its effect if the flow of a river is reduced and that is commonly done by extraction, to provide domestic and industrial water supplies, from points at or near the sources of rivers and their tributaries. By this means many rivers have been totally destroyed during the last thirty years. In Hertfordshire alone, every trout river has been destroyed in this way, and the country's largest river, the Lee, now consists entirely of sewage effluent.

Competition from other water sports and pastimes for water space has become increasingly severe. Waterskiing is especially damaging to angling interests, but the enormous increase in the ownership of motor cruisers has made fishing almost impossible on some rivers, particularly the Thames, and on the Norfolk Broads, during the daylight hours of summer. Such craft cause serious pollution, bylaws having proved quite incapable of preventing the emptying of chemical lavatories directly into the water.

Yet another serious and increasing threat to angling comes from ill-informed townspeople who wish to ban all field sports on the grounds that they are cruel. There can be little doubt that this movement has been and will be exploited by extreme left-wing political elements, whose concern with cruelty is non-existent but who imagine that field sports are pursued by idle, rich right-wingers and are to be deplored for that reason. I am in no doubt whatever that the Labour Party's threat to ban both fishing and shooting was dropped not from any change of heart but through fear of losing votes. There are other interests, involving the promotion of lucrative spectator sports like professional football, who would gladly see angling made illegal or curtailed, since it occupies the leisure of three million people who might otherwise pay to watch sport instead of participating.

The dangers to angling are thus formidable; if they are not defeated in the future, the reluctance by anglers to finance adequately their protecting representative bodies will be largely to blame.

What of future developments in facilities? Most rivers continue to deteriorate and that means more and more fishing in man-made stillwaters like reservoirs and wet pits produced by excavation of clay, gravel, and sand. This trend began half a century ago and still continues. Some of these stillwaters are regularly stocked with trout; the development by selective breeding of faster-growing strains of trout may assist materially in slowing down the escalation of stocking costs. Stillwaters are far less vulnerable to pollution, though many of them are being lost to angling because yachtsmen, water skiers, and powerboat enthusiasts are always able to obtain large sums in grant aid from public funds, that are for the most part denied to angling.

Capable management of angling waters is rare. Most angling organizations remain committed to the belief that heavy stocking is the answer when the sport provided by any water deteriorates. The result is starved fish, highly vulnerable to disease. The best hope for improvement lies in the activities of capable scientists employed by regional water authorities, whose numbers are fortunately increasing.

Over the centuries, no one has been able to predict great advances in tackle materials and design, yet many such advances have been made in recent years. The advent of carbon fibre as a rod material has shown that anglers generally are perfectly willing to pay a good deal more for a superior article, which ought to encourage the tackle trade to continue with its research and development. While I cannot visualize any startling improvements, I have no doubt they will be made.

As the number of anglers increases, as it will unless the politicians and others who wish to ban angling have their way, it may prove necessary to ration fishing on a time basis. This is already done in some trout fisheries, where an angler may be allocated one or more days in each week. I predict that some similar system will have to be applied to some, if not all, coarse fishing waters, many of which are already grossly over-fished and over-crowded.

It is even possible, if anglers change their attitude and provide the necessary money, that rivers now destroyed by pollution and abstraction will be recovered, so that more angling space will become available, but it is unlikely to keep pace with the increased demand.

I cannot, therefore, paint a rosy picture for the future of angling; but I think that it will continue, albeit in a curtailed form, for many centuries to come. Whether that prediction proves correct depends to a great extent upon what anglers do to help themselves.

Appendix: Tying a good knot

Reliable knots can make the vital difference between landing or losing the fish of a lifetime.

In Fig A this commonly-used knot for spade-end hooks is less reliable than the knot in Fig B. The first knot is liable to slip and pull free under pressure. In Fig C the reliable knot is tightened and slid along the shank. The more pressure applied to the line the more tightly the knot will grip the hook shank.

Fig D shows an equally reliable knot for tying eyed hooks or swivel eyes. Eyed hooks are commonly used in the larger sizes with thick nylon to match. This knot gives far more grip and reliability than a tucked half-blood knot.

Fig E shows a similar knot for joining two strands.

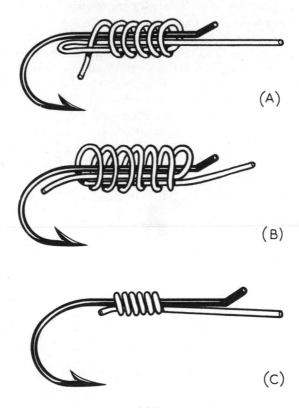

(A)

(B)

(C)

(D)

(E)

(A) A common but unreliable knot for spade end hooks
(B) A thoroughly reliable knot for spade end hooks
(C) Knot B tightened. It is then slid up to spade
(D) Grinner knot (to hook or swivel)
(E) Double grinner knot (joining two strands)

Acknowledgments

All the chapters in this book, except for the last, were originally published in *Angling Times* as follows:
1, 17 Oct 68; 2, 10 Aug 67; 3, 10 Jul 64; 4, 27 Mar 64; 5, 3 Jan 64; 6, 25 Feb 76; 7, 4 Jun 54; 8, 13 May 55; 9, 13 Sept 63; 10, 10 Aug 62; 11, 21 May 54; 12, 20 May 60; 13, 22 Jul 55; 14, 13 May 71; 15, 2 Dec 55; 16, 28 Jan 55; 17, 8 Apr 55; 18, 30 Jun 76; 19, 31 May 63; 20, 4 Jan 57; 21, 28 Aug 64; 22, 5 Jul 63; 23, 4 Feb 66; 24, 31 Jul 74; 25, 31 Jul 69; 26, 20 Nov 69; 27, 16 Apr 75; 28, 3 Nov 76; 29, 18 Jun 70; 30, 3 Jul 64; 31, 14 Jun 63; 32, 7 Oct 55; 33, 24 Nov 76; 34, 8 Feb 57; 35, 3 Sep 54; 36, 1 Oct 54; 37, 14 Jun 63; 38, 4 Oct 63; 39, 10 May 63; 40, 13 Feb 69; 41, 20 Aug 75; 42, 12 Oct 62; 43, 28 Nov 58; 44, 17 Mar 76; 45, 20 Nov 64; 46, 6 May 71; 47, 14 Jan 76; 48, 18 Jan 68; 49, first published here.